Discovering Iceland: Your Travel Guide

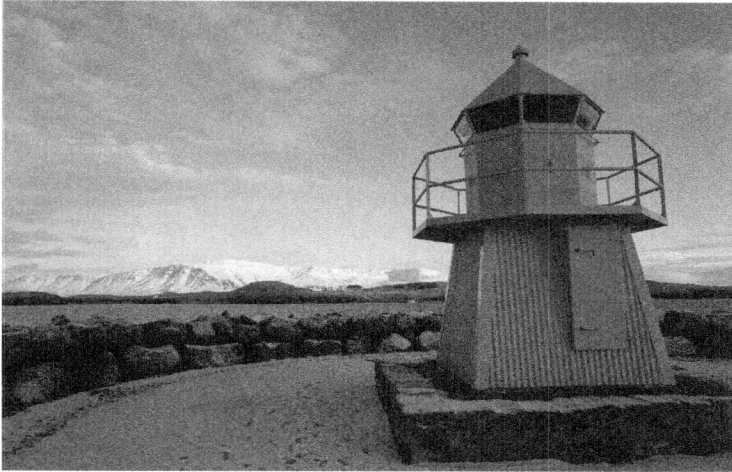

Your Gateway to Untamed Beauty and Adventure

JOHNSON WALKER

2

Table Of Content

Chapter 1

- A Comprehensive Guide to Planning an Unforgettable Trip to Iceland.
- Essential Packing Guide for Your Visit to Iceland and Suggested Items to Buy.

Chapter 2

- Visa and Entry Requirements into Iceland Custom Recommendations and Visa Application.
- Dos and Don'ts of Iceland You should Never Forget.

Chapter 3

- **Safety Requirements:
  Providing a Safe and Enjoyable Visit to
  Iceland Safety Requirements.**

Chapter 4

- **Money and Budgeting for an Affordable
  Vacation in Iceland: A Comprehensive
  Guide to Saving and Targeted Budgeting.**

Chapter 5

- **Arriving in Iceland**

Chapter 6

- **Transportation Options in Iceland:
  Budgeting for Car Rental and Owning
  Your Own Car OnTour.**

Chapter 7

- **The Rules Instructions on Iceland Laws and Ethics for Visitors.**

Chapter 8

- **Iceland Cultural Events and Festivals.**

Chapter 9

- **Accommodation Options in Iceland: Budgeting for Rental Homestay and Hotels.**

Chapter 10

- **Best Time to Visit Iceland for Perfect Weather And Memorable Experiences.**

Chapter 11

- **Iceland Top Tourist Destinations You Must See.**

Chapter 12

- **Dining and entertainment restaurants in Iceland.**

Chapter 13

- **Hidden Gems in Iceland: A Treasure Hunt Through Its Unknown Gems.**

Chapter 14

- **Souvenir Shopping in Iceland**

Chapter 15

- **Tips and Essential Information for Travelers Visiting Iceland**

Introduction

"Discovering Iceland: Your Ultimate Travel Guide" welcomes you on a remarkable excursion to a place that is known for stunning scenes, dynamic culture, and untamed regular excellence. Iceland, a distant island settled in the North Atlantic, has spellbound voyagers for a really long time with its captivating blend of geothermal miracles, flowing cascades, ice sheets, and an unrivaled divine presentation of Aurora Borealis. In this extensive travel guide, we'll dig profound into the core of this Nordic pearl, giving you all that you really want to design the experience that could only be described as epic.

The excursion to find Iceland starts with an investigation of its remarkable scenes molded by volcanic action. The island, frequently alluded to as the "Place that is known for Fire and Ice," flaunts a different landscape set apart by ice sheets, fountains, natural aquifers, and transcending volcanoes. Specialists dig into the geographical cycles that have shaped this powerful climate, unwinding the insider facts of Iceland's structural plate limits and the unique exchange of earth's powers.

Past its geographical charm, Iceland offers a social embroidery woven with old practices and a versatile soul. The Icelandic adventures, legendary stories of legends and divine beings, give a window into the country's past, offering bits of knowledge into its fables and verifiable accounts. Researchers take part in the investigation of these adventures, uncovering the complicated associations between writing, folklore, and the aggregate character of the Icelandic public.

The disclosure of Iceland stretches out past its regular and social aspects to envelop logical exploration in different disciplines. Researchers investigate the extraordinary environments that flourish in outrageous circumstances, from the strong vegetation to the plentiful birdlife that populates waterfront bluffs. In the meantime, environment researchers direct their concentration toward the Icy district, involving Iceland as a point of convergence for understanding the effects of environmental change on high-scope conditions.

As scientists dive into the profundities of Iceland's geographical past and social legacy, they add to a more extensive comprehension of the World's elements and the perplexing exchange among nature and human social orders. The excursion to find Iceland is a complex investigation, winding around together strings of geography, humanities, writing, and natural science to disentangle the secrets of this enrapturing island at the edge of the Cold Circle.

The appeal of Iceland stretches out into the domain of natural supportability and sustainable power. This island country remains as a worldwide model in bridling the force of its regular assets for economical turn of events. Scientists dig into Iceland's spearheading utilization of geothermal and hydropower energy, investigating how these sources have formed the country's energy scene as well as impacted worldwide discussions on green innovation and maintainability.

Besides, the disclosure of Iceland includes an assessment of its extraordinary socio-political setting. With a populace known for its versatility and imagination, Iceland has endured monetary difficulties and gone through cultural changes. Researchers dissect the Icelandic model of administration, its accentuation on orientation balance, and the effect of such factors on molding a moderate and comprehensive society.

The investigation of Iceland additionally reaches out to the divine domain, as the country's area makes it an optimal spot for noticing Aurora Borealis. Astrophysicists and stargazers run to Iceland to concentrate on the auroras, opening the secrets of these amazing light shows and their association with sun powered movement.

In the abstract domain, the tradition of Icelandic writing rises above the antiquated adventures. Contemporary creators draw motivation from the scene and social legacy, causing a dynamic scholarly situation that reflects both the immortal and current parts of Icelandic character. The investigation of Icelandic writing turns into an excursion through time, investigating the progression and development of narrating in this powerful island country.

Basically, finding Iceland is a multidisciplinary odyssey, winding around together strings of geophysics, nature, human science, stargazing, and writing. This diverse investigation adds to scholastic information as well as encourages a profound appreciation for the interconnectedness of nature, culture, and human resourcefulness in this place that is known for differences and marvels.

Whether you're a brave climber, an untamed life fan, a set of experiences buff, or a social wayfarer, "Finding Iceland" takes care of each and every sort of voyager. With adroit tips on transportation, facilities, eating, and pressing, we intend to make your excursion consistent and significant. As you flip through these pages, get ready to leave on an odyssey through a place that is known for Vikings, mythical people, and unmatched scenes. Iceland anticipates, and this guide is your definitive identification to an extraordinary encounter.

In "Discovering Iceland: Your Ultimate Travel Guide," we take you past the very much trampled ways and vacationer areas of interest, offering insider information and functional exhortation to assist you with making a customized schedule. Whether you fantasize about investigating ice caves, setting out on an icy mass climb, or absorbing a distant natural aquifer, our side is your compass to making those fantasies a reality.

To really see the value in Iceland's enchantment, we'll disentangle the country's extraordinary culture, diving into its creative legacy, culinary enjoyments, and the strong soul of its kin. You'll find the old stories and legends that have molded the Icelandic personality and the contemporary workmanship scene that is thriving in this remote corner of the world.

The book likewise incorporates fundamental data about when to visit, how to get ready for Iceland's always evolving climate, and the best times to observe the magical Aurora Borealis dance across the Cold sky. Pragmatic tips for frugal explorers and families are given, guaranteeing that Iceland can be an objective for everybody, no matter what your movement style or spending plan.

In this way, whether you're arranging a short escape or a drawn out experience, "Discovering Iceland" is your extensive manual for a nation where nature rules, where icy masses meet volcanoes, and where the limits among the real world and fantasy obscure. Allow this book to be your vital aspect for opening the miracles of Iceland, a spot that guarantees a genuinely extraordinary excursion.

<u>Overview</u>

Iceland, an entrancing island country in the North Atlantic Sea, is known for its dazzling regular excellence and remarkable social legacy. Iceland's amicable mix of regular miracles, rich history, and moderate society make it a genuinely enamoring objective, drawing in voyagers from everywhere the world to encounter its sorcery. Whether you look for experience or peacefulness, Iceland brings something to the table for everybody.

Topography: Iceland is a place that is known for emotional differences, with volcanoes, glacial masses, fountains, and cascades coinciding as one. It rides the Mid-Atlantic Edge, making it a topographically dynamic locale. The nation's scene is set apart by rough mountains, fjords, and a tremendous good country level.

Environment: Notwithstanding its name, Iceland's environment is milder than one could anticipate, because of the warming impact of the North Atlantic Current. Summers are cool, with long light hours,

16

while winters can be cold and dim. The nation is
known for its erratic climate.

Culture: Iceland's way of life is well established in
its Norse legacy. The Icelandic adventures, old
accounts of valor and experience, assume a huge
part in the country's personality. The language,
Icelandic, is firmly connected with Old Norse and
has changed moderately minimal throughout the
long term. The nation has a flourishing expressions
scene, with writing, music, and visual expressions
being conspicuous.

Economy: Iceland's economy is assorted, with
businesses going from fishing and aluminum
creation to the travel industry and sustainable power.
The nation is known for its obligation to efficient
power energy, with a huge part of its power coming
from geothermal and hydropower sources.

The travel industry: Iceland has seen a flood in the
travel industry lately, because of its stunning regular
attractions. Guests come to observe the Aurora
Borealis, investigate the Brilliant Circle's
geothermal marvels, wash in the Blue Tidal pond,
and travel through the good countries. The country's

perfect wilderness offers valuable open doors for climbing, glacial mass visits, and that's just the beginning.

Natural life: Iceland is home to an assortment of natural life, including puffins, reindeer, and seals. Birdwatching is famous, and the oceans encompassing Iceland are wealthy in marine life. Whales, both humpback and orca, are ordinarily spotted on whale-watching visits.

History: Iceland's set of experiences is an adventure of Viking settlement, middle age clan leaders, and an exceptional parliamentary custom. In 930 Promotion, the Althing, one of the world's most seasoned parliaments, was laid out. Iceland acquired freedom from Denmark in 1944 and is presently a sovereign country.

Experience: The nation offers endless open doors for experience, from ice climbing and snowmobiling to horseback riding and investigating ice caves. The normal excellence of Iceland gives a steadily changing background to open air aficionados.

Environment:

In spite of its name, Iceland encounters a milder environment than one could expect, because of the warming impact of the Bay Stream. Winters can be cold, and summers are moderately cool. The weather conditions can be capricious, yet it adds to the nation's charm.

Culture and History:
Iceland's way of life is well established in Norse practices and folklore. The Icelandic Adventures, written in the thirteenth hundred years, are fundamental for its artistic legacy. The nation acquired freedom from Denmark in 1944 and has areas of strength for any public character.

Capital and Urban communities:
Reykjavik, the capital and biggest city, is the social and monetary center of Iceland. Different towns and urban communities, like Akureyri and Egilsstaðir, offer exceptional encounters and admittance to the country's regular miracles.

The travel industry:
Iceland's amazing regular magnificence draws sightseers from around the world. Famous attractions incorporate the Blue Tidal pond, Brilliant

Circle, Vatnajökull Public Park, and Aurora Borealis. Open air exercises like climbing, icy mass traveling, and geothermal washing are pervasive.

Untamed life:
Iceland's separation has prompted an extraordinary environment. You can track down puffins, icy foxes, and reindeer, while the waters overflow with marine life like whales and seals.

Language:
Icelandic is the authority language, and most Icelanders are conversant in English. This makes it somewhat simple for explorers to impart.

Economy:
Iceland's economy depends on fishing, geothermal energy, and progressively, the travel industry. It's known for its sustainable power sources, using geothermal and hydropower widely.

Challenges:
The nation faces ecological issues like soil disintegration and the protection of its sensitive biological systems. Overseeing the travel industry reasonably is likewise a critical test

Aurora Borealis (Aurora Borealis):
Iceland is quite possibly the best spot on the planet to observe the hypnotizing Aurora Borealis. The dull winter evenings, combined with its area close to the Icy Circle, give ideal circumstances to this normal light showcase.

Underground aquifers and Geothermal Action:
Iceland is dabbed with various geothermal natural aquifers. The Blue Tidal pond is the most popular, yet there are numerous others, both notable and unlikely treasures, where you can absorb normally warmed waters.

Public Parks:
Iceland flaunts a few staggering public parks, including Thingvellir, Vatnajökull, and Snæfellsjökull. These parks protect the country's remarkable scenes, from break valleys to icy masses.

Experience Exercises:
For daredevils, Iceland offers a large number of exercises, including glacial mass climbing, ice buckling, snowmobiling, and in any event, plunging between structural plates in Silfra Gap.

Cooking:
Icelandic cooking frequently rotates around privately obtained fixings. Conventional dishes incorporate sheep, fish, and dairy items. Try not to pass up on the opportunity to attempt one of a kind food sources like matured shark and rye bread prepared utilizing geothermal intensity.

12 PM Sun:
In the late spring months, especially around the mid-year solstice, Iceland encounters the peculiarity of the "12 PM sun." This implies 24-hour light, considering expanded investigation.

Language and Training:
Iceland has a profoundly proficient and knowledgeable populace. The nation puts major areas of strength for schooling, and it's home to one of the world's most established parliaments, the Althing, established in 930 Promotion.

Security:

Iceland is viewed as quite possibly the most secure country on the planet, with low crime percentages and a solid feeling of local area.

Transportation:
The Ring Street (Highway 1) is a well known method for investigating the country by street, offering a total circuit around Iceland. The nation likewise has a very much associated homegrown flight organization.

Brief History Of Iceland

Iceland, a remote and rough island country in the North Atlantic, flaunts a rich and exceptional history that traverses more than a thousand years. From its underlying settlement by Norse travelers to its cutting edge status as a flourishing Scandinavian country, Iceland's set of experiences is a story of strength, development, and social character.

Iceland's set of experiences started with the appearance of Norse pilgrims in the late ninth 100 years. Driven by figures like Ingólfur Arnarson and Erik the Red, these Viking pioneers laid out the main super durable settlements on the island. The adventures, awe-inspiring accounts of this period, recount the narratives of their battles, investigation, and early administration. The Althing, laid out in 930 CE, is much of the time thought about as the world's most established parliamentary foundation, denoting a critical crossroads in Iceland's political history.

One of the most basic defining moments in Icelandic history was its transformation to Christianity in the mid eleventh 100 years. This change was generally tranquil and was started by conspicuous tribal leaders like Ólafur Tryggvason. The progress from agnostic to Christianity significantly affected Iceland's way of life and legislative issues, as it associated the island all the more near Europe.

Iceland during this period was portrayed by an exceptional arrangement of administration known as the "Althing Ward." The Althing, the public get together, assumed a critical part in navigation and compromise. This period likewise saw the prospering of Icelandic writing, with adventures and Eddic verse turning into the signs of Icelandic culture. Adventures like Njála and Egil's Adventure gave a window into the existences of early Icelanders.

By the thirteenth 100 years, the Althing District was confronting inward difficulty and outside dangers, including regional questions and the impact of the Norwegian crown. Iceland's tribal leaders in the long run swore their unwavering ness to the Lord of Norway, acquiring the island under Norwegian rule

1262-1264. This association denoted the end of Iceland's autonomy, and it later fell under Danish rule in the seventeenth 100 years.

Iceland's battle for freedom from Danish rule was a delayed interaction. It started in the nineteenth hundred years with public arousing and bit by bit picking up speed. In 1918, Iceland turned into a sovereign state in an individual association with the Lord of Denmark. This plan ultimately developed, prompting full freedom on December 1, 1918. The Realm of Iceland was laid out, and in 1944, it turned into a republic, formally disavowing Denmark.

Since acquiring full freedom, Iceland has changed into a cutting edge, prosperous, and majority rule country. The mid-twentieth century saw the extension of its economy, especially through fisheries and the use of geothermal energy. In late many years, Iceland plays had a functioning impact in foreign relations, turning into an individual from different associations, including NATO and the Unified Countries.

Iceland is known for its obligation to ecological maintainability and environmentally friendly power sources, bridling its geothermal and hydroelectric potential. Furthermore, the nation has left a huge imprint in human expression, creating globally acclaimed performers, scholars, and producers.

All in all, Iceland's set of experiences is a demonstration of the perseverance of a little island country and its kin. From the age of the Vikings to the current day, the Icelanders have kept an unmistakable social personality while embracing the difficulties and chances of the cutting edge world. Iceland's rich history keeps on forming its special person and worldwide standing.

Five Killer Apps

Stræto App:

The Stræto Application is a versatile application that fills in as a far reaching device for public transportation in Iceland, explicitly in the Reykjavik metropolitan region. It is intended to make driving and going inside the capital and its encompassing locales more advantageous and proficient.

The Stræto Application is basically evolved to give data and administrations connected with the public transportation framework in Reykjavik and nearby towns. This incorporates transports, cable cars, and ships, which are all essential for the Stræto organization.

The Application additionally has key highlights like...

Constant Following: Where clients can follow the ongoing area of transports and cable cars to know when their next vehicle will show up at a particular stop.

Course Arranging: The application offers a course organizer that assists clients with tracking down the most productive method for getting started with one area then onto the next utilizing the Strætó organization.

Admission Data: It gives subtleties on ticket costs and choices for different kinds of travelers, like grown-ups, seniors, youngsters, and vacationers.

Ticket Buy: Travelers can buy tickets straightforwardly through the application, which dispenses with the requirement for paper tickets and money installments ready.

Administration Cautions: Clients get notices about assistance disturbances, delays, and other significant updates.

Top choices and History: The application permits clients to save most loved courses or stops for speedy access and view their movement history.

Þjóðskrá App:

The Þjóðskrá application, otherwise called the Public Vault application, is an Icelandic versatile application that gives admittance to different taxpayer supported organizations and individual data. It permits Icelandic residents to get to their authority archives, for example, birth declarations, marriage authentications, and that's just the beginning. Clients can likewise change their legitimate location and view significant information from the Public Vault. The application offers comfort and effectiveness in managing official records and taxpayer supported organizations, making it a significant device for occupants of Iceland.

Safetravel Iceland App:
The SafeTravel Iceland Application is a versatile application intended to improve the wellbeing and experience of voyagers visiting Iceland. It gives data and assets to assist explorers with exploring the nation's novel and frequently testing common habitat. The application offers elements, for example, ongoing climate and street condition refreshes, crisis contact data, and the capacity to submit itinerary items and get area based cautions. Voyagers can utilize the application to remain informed about possible perils and remain protected while investigating Iceland's shocking scenes.

The SafeTravel Iceland Application possess key highlights like..
Climate and Street Conditions: The application gives ongoing weather conditions updates and street

conditions, assisting explorers with settling on informed conclusions about their excursions. This is vital in Iceland's always evolving environment.

Security Alarms: Clients can get area based cautions and notices about climate admonitions, cataclysmic events, or other well being related data intended for their movement region.

Travel Arranging: Voyagers can enter their itinerary items, including objections and agenda, to illuminate specialists and get help if necessary. This element guarantees that somebody knows your whereabouts if there should be an occurrence of a crisis.

Crisis Administrations: The application offers direct admittance to crisis contacts, including the Icelandic Pursuit and Salvage groups and clinical benefits, permitting clients to rapidly call for help.

Intelligent Guide: It incorporates an intuitive guide with data about neighboring attractions, facilities, and administrations, making it simpler to investigate Iceland.

Wellbeing Rules: The application gives rules and data on the most proficient method to remain protected while going in Iceland, particularly in the country's one of a kind common habitat.

Disconnected Openness: A few highlights are accessible disconnected, which can be useful in distant regions with restricted web networks.

Tix.is:
Tix.is is an Icelandic tagging application that permits clients to handily find, buy, and oversee tickets for different occasions, including motion pictures, shows, and exhibitions. With an easy to understand interface, it gives a consistent encounter to occasion participants, offering data about forthcoming occasions, seat choice, and secure internet based ticket exchanges. The application plans to improve on the ticket-purchasing cycle and upgrade the general occasion going experience for its clients in Iceland.

Tix.is likewise furnishes clients with customized proposals in light of their inclinations, making it more straightforward to investigate new occasions

and find unlikely treasures. The application
frequently includes selective arrangements and early
admittance to tickets, making added incentive for its
clients. Moreover, Tix.is consolidates a helpful
computerized tagging framework, killing the
requirement for actual tickets and smoothing out
section processes at occasions. By and large, it's a
complete stage taking special care of the different
diversion needs of its crowd in Iceland.

Krónan:
The Krónan application is a helpful device for those
in Iceland. It permits clients to peruse items, make
shopping records, and even offers advancements.
With an easy to understand interface, it improves on
the shopping for food experience at Krónan stores.

You can utilize the Krónan application to find the
closest store, actually take a look at item
accessibility, and access customized limits. It's a
useful ally for smoothing out your staple preparation
and improving the general shopping process.

Furthermore, the Krónan application frequently
gives refreshes on exceptional offers and permits

clients to arrange food for home conveyance or pickup helpfully. It consistently coordinates innovation into the shopping for food schedule, making it more effective and customized to individual inclinations.

The application's point of interaction is intended for a simple route, guaranteeing a problem free encounter. Clients can investigate a large number of items, including new produce, storage room staples, and family things. The capacity to follow expenses and oversee shopping history adds one more layer of comfort for clients hoping to keep steady over their staple spending plan. You can download the Krónan application from the Application Store for iOS gadgets or Google Play for Android gadgets.

Chapter 1

A Comprehensive Guide to Planning an Unforgettable Trip to Iceland.

Orchestrating a trip to Iceland is an undeniably exhilarating endeavor that involves stunning scenes and intriguing experiences. From the heavenly greatness of its icy masses to the exuberant culture of Reykjavik, Iceland has something for every explorer. Arranging an outing to Iceland likewise incorporates a balance among preparation and quickness. Embrace the unanticipated, whether it's a mystery overflow or an open door experience with very much arranged neighborhood individuals.

Begin by researching Iceland's attractions, environment, and activities. Make a versatile timetable that covers must-see places like the Splendid Circle, Blue Lagoon, and Jökulsárlón Chilly mass Lagoon.
Consider the length of your excursion, recollecting that Iceland offers different experiences in both summer and winter.

Iceland's atmospheric conditions can be strange, so pack layers, waterproof dress, and intense footwear. Summer (June to August) offers long days and milder temperatures, ideal for researching. Winter (December to February) conveys more restricted days yet a chance to notice Aurora Borealis.

Book offices early, especially during top seasons. Decisions range from lodgings in Reykjavik to guesthouses and cabins in extra far away districts. Consider staying in different regions to experience the various scenes Iceland offers that might be of some value.

Renting a vehicle is the most versatile technique for researching Iceland. Ensure your rental vehicle suits your schedule things, especially expecting that you mean to meander into the great countries.On the other hand, composed visits can give a supportive strategy for seeing notable attractions in case you would truly prefer not to drive.

Iceland can be costly, so plan your spending plan fittingly. Address accommodation, galas, transportation, and activities.

Look for monetary arrangement all around arranged decisions, for instance, stores for feasts and free attractions like fountains and normal springs.

English is comprehensively spoken, simplifying correspondence. Regardless, learning several Icelandic articulations can redesign your experience. The money is the Icelandic Króna (ISK). Mastercards are comprehensively recognized, but having some cash for additional unassuming foundations is perfect.

Iceland is an image taker's paradise. Be prepared with a fair camera and extra batteries, especially if chasing after Aurora Borealis. Respect nature by following the "leave no follow" standard and avoiding bound areas.
End:
Recollect the Splendid Circle for your timetable, including Þingvellir Recreational area, Geysir Geothermal District, and Gullfoss Outpouring. These outstanding objections offer a short investigate Iceland's territory contemplates.

Make an effort not to miss the relaxing experience of retaining geothermal underground springs. While the Blue Lagoon is notable, research other normal showers like the Strange Lagoon or Myvatn Nature Showers.

Iceland is home to grouped untamed life, including puffins and seals. Consider taking a boat visit to perceive these creatures or visit unequivocal locales like Dyrhólaey and Jökulsárlón for untamed life photography. On account of visiting in winter, it is an irrefutable need to seek after Aurora Borealis. Check the aurora measure, experience away from city lights, and show limitation for a potential chance to notice the spellbinding dance of the auroras.

Endeavor standard Icelandic dishes like sheep stew, fish, and the well known hotdog. Embrace the local food scene in Reykjavik, where you'll find various diners offering new, close by trimmings.

If setting out on a journey, ensure your vehicle is ready for Icelandic conditions. Check road conditions regularly, and be prepared for various scenes, from dim sand coastlines to cold mountain passes.

Ponder camping out for a more clear contribution in nature. Iceland's enjoying nature regions give workplaces, and arousing enveloped by astounding scene is an involvement with itself.

Experience the characteristic of the 12 PM Sun all through the pre-summer months. Value extended light hours, considering exceptional activities like 12 PM sun climbs or late-night photography.

Bring back a piece of Iceland by searching for veritable tokens. Consider things like Icelandic woolens, hand custom-made claims to fame, or even a volcanic stone as a unique gift.

While organizing is basic, leave space for abruptness. Most likely the best experiences in Iceland can be unconstrained, like tracking down a mystery overflow or participating in a local event.

Practice able the movement business by with respect to the fragile environment. Stick to doled out trails, make an effort not to agitate untamed life, and know about the impact of your visit on Iceland's perfect nature. Although Iceland's atmospheric conditions can change rapidly. Be prepared for storm, wind, and even snow, especially accepting going during shoulder seasons. Checking atmospheric conditions guesses regularly will help you with changing your courses of action similarly.

Past the real superbness, endeavor to get the encapsulation of Iceland — the quietness, the sensation of involvement, and the extraordinary blend of typical powers that make this island a truly astounding goal.

Orchestrating a trip to Iceland isn't just about ticking off achievements anyway soaking yourself in a vast expanse of separations and wonders.

Essential Packing Guide for Your Visit to Iceland and Suggested Items to Buy.

Visiting Iceland is a stunning experience, where magnificent scenes and regular miracles anticipate every step of the way. As you set out on this Nordic excursion, careful pressing is fundamental to guarantee you're ready for the exceptional difficulties and encounters Iceland brings to the table. From the steadily changing climate to the captivating social revelations.

Waterproof Coat and Jeans: Iceland's weather conditions can be unusual. A solid, waterproof coat and jeans will protect you from downpour and wind, keeping you dry and warm during open air undertakings.

Protecting Layers: Pack warm or downy layers to remain warm in cooler temperatures. Layering is critical, permitting you to conform to changing atmospheric conditions.

Fleece or Engineered Base Layers: Long-sleeved warm tops and bottoms give extra protection. Fleece is especially viable in holding heat, in any event, when wet.

Solid Waterproof Boots: Agreeable, waterproof boots are fundamental for investigating Iceland's different territories, including icy masses, volcanic scenes, and sloppy paths.

Gloves, Cap, and Scarf: Safeguard furthest points with waterproof gloves, a warm cap, and a scarf. These frill are significant for remaining agreeable in cold circumstances.

Bathing suit: Remember a bathing suit for a remarkable Icelandic encounter - loosening up in geothermal natural aquifers or swimming in the Blue Tidal pond.

Knapsack: A strong, waterproof rucksack is fundamental for conveying your basics during roadtrips. Guarantee it's agreeable for broadened use.

Camera and Optics: Iceland offers dazzling vistas and natural life. Catch these minutes with a quality camera and optics for bird watching or spotting far off scenes.

Power Bank and Connectors: Keep gadgets accused of a dependable power bank. Iceland utilizes the Europlug (Type C and F) outlets, so bring reasonable connectors.

Journeying Shafts: On the off chance that you intend to climb, consider bringing traveling shafts for solidness and backing, particularly on lopsided territories.

Headlamp or Spotlight: Iceland encounters long winter evenings. A headlamp or spotlight is significant for exploring in obscurity or investigating caves.

Sunscreen and Lip Analgesic: Regardless of the cool temperatures, the sun can be extraordinary. Safeguard your skin with high SPF sunscreen and saturate your lips with an emollient.

Reusable Water Jug: Remain hydrated with a reusable water bottle. Iceland's water is unadulterated and protected to drink from taps.

Travel-sized Toiletries: Pack travel-sized cleanser, conditioner, and different toiletries to save space in your gear.

Medical aid Pack: Incorporate essential clinical supplies like pain killers, gauzes, and any private prescriptions.

Money and Charge cards: While cards are broadly acknowledged, it's wise to convey some money, particularly while heading out to distant regions.

Travel Protection: Guarantee you have far reaching travel protection that covers health related crises, trip undoings, and unforeseen occasions.

Guide and Manual: While GPS is helpful, having an actual guide and manual can be significant, giving extra experiences and data.

Reusable Shopping Pack: Iceland puts areas of strength for an on ecological manageability. Bring a reusable shopping pack to limit plastic utilization.

Diversion: Pack a book, tablet, or music player for diversion during long excursions or calm nights.

Snacks: Convey a few snacks to fuel yourself between feasts, particularly on the off chance that you intend to investigate distant regions.

Travel Pad and Cover: Remain open to during lengthy drives or trips with a minimized travel cushion and cover.

Ziploc Packs: Keep electronic gadgets and significant reports dry by putting away them in Ziploc packs.

Chapter 2

Visa and Entry Requirements into Iceland Custom Recommendations and Visa Application.

Iceland is the most meagerly populated country in Europe, with a populace of just 368,792 and an area of 103,000 km2. Two third of Iceland's populace is packed in Reykjavík, which is its capital and biggest city.

And also Iceland is a place that is known for supernatural scenes and dynamic culture, coaxes voyagers from across the globe. To set out on this Nordic experience, understanding the complexities of Iceland's visa and passage prerequisites is principal.

Visa Essentials:

Iceland is an individual from the Schengen Region, working on movement for guests from Schengen nations. Notwithstanding, for those external this zone, getting a Schengen visa is an essential. The Schengen visa permits passage into any of the 26

Schengen nations, including Iceland, for a short stay of as long as 90 days inside a 180-day time span.

For those proposing to work or concentrate on in Iceland, an alternate arrangement of visa guidelines applies. Work grants and understudy visas require extra documentation, like a letter of business or acknowledgment from an Icelandic foundation. Understanding the particular prerequisites for each kind of visa is fundamental to guarantee a smooth application process.

Custom Recommendations:

Prior to jumping into the visa application process, familiarizing oneself with Iceland's customs is astute. The Icelandic public invest wholeheartedly in their rich legacy and warm friendliness. Embracing neighborhood customs, for example, addressing individuals by their most memorable names and sticking to reliability, improves the general travel insight.

Investigating Iceland's novel cooking is an unquestionable necessity. From customary dishes like hákarl (matured shark) to the delightful Icelandic sheep, enjoying nearby flavors gives a culinary excursion that supplements the grand scenes.

Visa Application

Decide the Kind of Visa: Distinguish the motivation behind your visit to Iceland (e.g., the travel industry, business, study). Different visa types have explicit prerequisites, so pick the one that best suits your requirements.

Really take a look at Qualification: Guarantee you meet the qualification rules for the picked visa class.

Really look at the length and motivation behind the visa to line up with your itinerary items.

Application Structure: Get the proper visa application structure from the authority site or the Icelandic international safe haven/department. Finish up the structure precisely and totally.

Supporting Reports: Accumulate important archives, for example, identification, visa estimated photographs, travel agenda, confirmation of convenience, and travel protection. Business explorers could require a letter of greeting, while understudies might require an acknowledgment letter from an Icelandic instructive organization.

Monetary Evidence: Give proof of adequate assets to cover your visit in Iceland.This might incorporate bank proclamations, sponsorship letters, or a blend of both.

Travel Protection: Secure travel protection that covers clinical costs and bringing home however long your visit might last.

Language Prerequisites: Contingent upon the reason for your visit, you might have to show capability in Icelandic or English.

Application Accommodation: Present your application at the Icelandic government office or department in your country. A few nations might have a visa application focus where you can apply.

Visa Expense: Pay the expected visa expense. The sum shifts relying upon the sort and span of the visa.

Handling Time: Know about the handling time for visa applications.

Present your application well ahead of your arranged travel date.

Dos and Don'ts of Iceland You should Never Forget.

Iceland is a one of a kind and dazzling location, known for its normal excellence and energetic culture. To capitalize on your visit, it's essential to know about the customs that will guarantee a deferential and charming experience:

Dos:

Regard Nature: Follow assigned ways and trails to limit your effect on the sensitive Icelandic verdure.
Respect untamed life from a good ways and abstain from upsetting settling birds or seals.

Embrace the Climate: Dress in layers and be ready for unusual climate, as it can change quickly.
Check weather conditions figures and street conditions consistently, particularly during winter.
Natural aquifers Behavior:

On the off chance that you intend to visit natural aquifers, shower completely prior to entering to keep up with their neatness. Regard neighborhood customs and rules in regards to fitting swimwear and conduct.

Follow Leave No Follow Standards: Pack out the entirety of your junk and be aware of garbage removal, keeping the climate flawless.
Leave regular and verifiable locales as you tracked down them, saving Iceland's interesting scenes.

Reliability: Be on time for visits, trips, and other booked exercises to stay away from disturbances.
Regard the hour of local people and individual explorers, as reliability is profoundly esteemed.

Civility to Local people: Welcome local people with a well disposed "Góðan daginn" (Great day) and be pleasant in all connections. Request consent prior to taking photographs of individuals, particularly in provincial regions.

Investigate Neighborhood Food: Attempt customary Icelandic dishes like hákarl (matured shark) or skyr (yogurt). Support neighborhood organizations and partake in the different culinary contributions.

Don'ts:

Rough terrain Driving: Never adventure off stamped streets. Rough terrain driving is completely restricted and can harm the delicate climate.
Remain on assigned ways, even in regions without vegetation, to forestall soil disintegration.

Problematic Way of behaving at Cascades: Try not to move over wellbeing boundaries at cascades, as this can be perilous and impolite to the regular environmental elements.
Observe signage and rules to guarantee a protected and charming experience.

Littering: Never abandon litter. Iceland's perfect nature ought to be safeguarded for people in the future. Discard squander appropriately and use reusing offices.

Wild Setting up camp Limitations: Try not to wild camp in precluded regions or on confidential land without authorization. Really get to know setting up camp guidelines and utilize assigned camping areas when accessible.

Moving toward Natural life: Try not to approach or take care of wild creatures. Keep a protected separation to try not to upset their regular way of behaving. Be especially careful around ponies, regarding their space and heeding any direction from proprietors.

Overlooking Climate Alerts: Try not to misjudge Iceland's climate. Regard admonitions and warnings to guarantee your wellbeing. Be ready for wind, downpour, and expected changes in weather patterns.

Chapter 3

Safety Requirements
Providing a Safe and Enjoyable Visit
Iceland Safety Requirements.

Iceland, a country famous for its stunning scenes and novel geographical elements, puts a high need on security prerequisites to guarantee the prosperity of its inhabitants and guests. The island country, arranged in the North Atlantic, is defenseless to different weather patterns and geographical exercises, requiring hearty security measures.

Iceland's wellbeing guidelines incorporate different viewpoints, including street security. The flighty climate and testing landscapes request adherence as far as possible, appropriate vehicle support, and the utilization of winter tires during explicit seasons. Furthermore, voyagers are urged to remain informed about weather conditions figures and street conditions, particularly in far off regions.

Weather patterns: Quick weather conditions changes are normal. Check solid gauges, street conditions, and the SafeTravel site prior to branching out. Winter conditions request proper apparel, including layers, waterproof stuff, and protected footwear.

Street Wellbeing: Iceland has testing street conditions, particularly in winter. Guarantee your vehicle is appropriate, furnished with winter tires, and consistently follow street signs. F thronged streets, are frequently rock streets, require four-wheel-drive vehicles. Actually look at their status and conditions prior to setting out on your excursion.

Search and Salvage: Illuminate somebody about your itinerary items, particularly if heading into distant regions. Iceland's pursuit and salvage groups are volunteer-based and crucial in crises.

Normal Risks: Regard wellbeing boundaries and rules close to land ponders, natural aquifers, and icy masses. Unusual regular occasions can present dangers.
Be wary around waterfront regions because of unexpected waves, and keep rules at famous places of interest.

Natural life Security: Stay away from natural life, particularly seals and settling birds. Really get to know rules on interfacing with Icelandic ponies to guarantee your security and theirs.

Wellbeing Safety measures: Guarantee you have travel protection covering clinical costs, including clearing if important. Dive more deeply into the area of drug stores and clinical offices, particularly in the event that you have explicit wellbeing concerns.

Ecological Obligation: Follow the "Leave No Follow" standards to safeguard Iceland's flawless climate.
Regard assigned trails to keep away from soil disintegration and safeguard fragile environments. Because of its land qualities, Iceland faces the gamble of cataclysmic events, including volcanic ejections and tremors. The Icelandic Meteorological Office screens seismic movement and gives early alerts. Departure plans are set up, and the Common Assurance Division facilitates reactions to possible crises.

Social Regard: Regard neighborhood customs and customs. Icelanders esteem their security and may have unwritten standards about private space and cooperation.

Learn essential Icelandic expressions to upgrade correspondence and show appreciation for the neighborhood culture.

Liquor Utilization: The lawful savoring age Iceland is 20. Know about your liquor utilization, and note serious areas of strength for that drinks are just sold in state-claimed stores. Public intoxication is disapproved of, so polish off liquor dependably.

Visit Administrator Consistence: While taking part in directed visits, guarantee that administrators are authorized and conform to somewhere safe guidelines.

Research surveys and request proposals to pick trustworthy visit organizations.

Fire Wellbeing: Regard fire boycotts and rules, particularly during dry periods. Open flames can represent a critical gamble to Iceland's vegetation.

Utilize assigned pit fire regions and follow security conventions while setting up camp.

Language Help: While English is broadly spoken, particularly in traveler regions, learning a couple of fundamental Icelandic expressions can upgrade your experience and correspondence with local people.

Dependable Driving: Observe speed cutoff points and traffic guidelines tirelessly. Iceland's streets can be testing, and dependable driving adds to by and large security. Pull over securely to permit quicker vehicles to pass on single-path streets.

Water Security: Iceland's waters, including natural aquifers and streams, can be deceivingly strong and cold. Keep security rules for swimming and washing. Be careful of changing tides and flows, particularly close to seaside regions.

In conclusion, Iceland's safety requirements reflect a comprehensive approach to mitigate the risks associated with its unique natural environment. Whether navigating the challenging terrains, enjoying geothermal wonders, or partaking in outdoor adventures, visitors and residents alike are encouraged to embrace a culture of responsibility and awareness to ensure a safe and enjoyable experience in this captivating country.

Chapter 4

Money and Budgeting for an Affordable Vacation in Iceland: A Comprehensive Guide to Saving and Targeted Budgeting.

Arranging a get-away to the stunning scenes of Iceland is an interesting undertaking, however it's fundamental to deal with your funds shrewdly to capitalize on your excursion. Making a thoroughly examined spending plan and carrying out ways to save cash can guarantee an important encounter without burning through every last cent.

This presentation will direct you through the basics of dealing with your funds for your Icelandic experience, remembering methods for setting aside cash and laying out a designated spending plan.

Setting a Sensible Financial plan: Start by deciding your general spending plan for the Iceland get-away. Consider costs like flights, convenience, transportation, feasts, exercises, and unexpected expenses. Research normal costs in Iceland to make a reasonable spending plan that lines up with your monetary capacities.

Go During Off-Pinnacle Seasons: Deciding to visit during off-top seasons can essentially decrease costs. Convenience and flights are much of the time more reasonable, and you'll have the additional advantage of encountering less groups, taking into consideration a more private investigation of Iceland's regular miracles.

Booking Ahead of time: Exploit timely riser limits by booking flights, convenience, and visits well ahead of time. This gets lower costs as well as gives genuine serenity realizing that significant parts of your outing are coordinated.

Convenience Choices: Investigate different convenience choices, from financial plan cordial lodgings to guesthouses and Airbnb. Furthermore, consider remaining in self-catering facilities to save money on eating costs by setting up a portion of your feasts.

Transportation Decisions: Leasing a vehicle gives you the adaptability to investigate Iceland at your own speed. Think about rental costs, choose eco-friendly vehicles, and book ahead of time for the best arrangements. Public transportation is likewise accessible and can be a practical choice for specific courses.

Dinner Arranging: Eating out in Iceland can be expensive. To oversee food costs, plan a few feasts ahead of time and buy tidbits or food from neighborhood stores. This permits you to relish Icelandic food while monitoring costs.

Cash Trade and Installment Strategies: Be aware of money trade rates and exchange charges. Consider utilizing charge cards with no unfamiliar exchange expenses, and pull out cash decisively to keep away from exorbitant ATM charges. Research the best techniques for your monetary circumstance.

Rainy day account: Incorporate a backup stash in your financial plan to represent unforeseen costs. It's generally shrewd to have a monetary cushion for unanticipated conditions or unconstrained open doors that might emerge during your outing.

Everyday Spending Cutoff points: Put forth everyday spending lines for stay affordable for you. This assists you with monitoring your costs and guarantees that you don't overspend on insignificant things.

Research Free and Minimal expense Exercises: Iceland offers a plenty of regular marvels and social encounters that won't cost a fortune. Research free or minimal expense exercises, like climbing trails, natural aquifers, and nearby occasions, to upgrade your get-away without stressing your spending plan.

Following Your Costs During the Excursion: When you're in Iceland, determinedly track your costs to remain acceptable for you. Use applications or a straightforward scratch pad to record each buy, including dinners, transportation, and trinkets. Routinely survey your spending against your underlying financial plan to guarantee you're keeping focused.

Bunch Travel and Shared Costs:
Consider going with companions or family to share costs on facilities, rental vehicles, and even feasts.

Bunch limits might be accessible for specific exercises, making it a more conservative choice contrasted with solo travel.

Use Public Conveniences: Exploit public conveniences, for example, underground aquifers and pools, which are socially advancing as well as cost not exactly some traveler driven attractions. Iceland has various geothermal pools, and numerous neighborhood pools are reasonable and offer a brief look into Icelandic regular routine.

Setting up camp Choices: For the gutsy explorer, setting up camp is a financial plan accommodating convenience decision. Iceland has various campgrounds, furnishing a potential chance to interface with nature and individual voyagers. Guarantee you have the proper stuff and actually look at occasional accessibility.

Careful Photography: While catching recollections is fundamental, be aware of photography costs. Consider buying a neighborhood SIM card with information for your cell phone as opposed to depending on costly worldwide wandering expenses. Moreover, research the best times for regular lighting to upgrade your photos without the requirement for costly camera gear.

Outside of what might be expected Investigation: Investigate less touristy locales to find unlikely treasures that are less packed as well as frequently more spending plan cordial. Leasing a vehicle and wandering into the field can prompt one of a kind encounters and beautiful scenes without the significant expenses related with well known vacationer locations.

Volunteer Open doors: Investigate volunteer open doors or social trade programs. A few associations offer food and lodging in return for charitable effort, giving a vivid encounter while essentially decreasing convenience costs.

Comprehensive developments and Celebrations: Actually take a look at the neighborhood schedule for widespread developments or celebrations during your visit. Taking part in local area occasions can offer a more profound comprehension of Icelandic culture and may incorporate free or minimal expense exercises, exhibitions, or presentations.

Pressing Basics: Pack carefully to keep away from pointless costs. Bring fundamentals like a reusable water container, snacks, and fitting dress for shifting weather patterns. Having these things close by can save you from rash spending on accommodation things during your movements.

Remain in Neighborhood Homes: Consider remaining in guesthouses or overnight boardinghouses worked by local people. These facilities frequently give a more customized insight for a portion of the expense of bigger lodgings. Drawing in with local people can likewise prompt important hints on spending plan cordial exercises and feasting choices.

Learn Essential Self-Protection: While Iceland is by and large protected, it's generally insightful to be ready. Learning essential self-preservation can support your certainty and assist you with exploring new regions effortlessly, possibly keeping away from circumstances that might prompt startling costs

All in all, a very much oversaw spending plan is the way to partaking in your Iceland excursion without pointless monetary pressure. By grasping the expenses, setting a practical spending plan, and carrying out compelling saving systems, you can capitalize on your Icelandic experience while remaining inside your monetary means.

Chapter 5

Arriving in Iceland

Arriving Iceland guarantees an enthralling mix of normal miracles, exceptional culture, and a dash of experience. Keflavík Global Air terminal, situated around 50 kilometers southwest of Reykjavik, is the principal passage for worldwide voyagers. As you land, the fresh Icelandic air quickly establishes the vibe for your Nordic experience.

Transportation choices from the air terminal to Reykjavik incorporate transport transports, taxicabs, and rental vehicles. The beautiful drive acquaints you with Iceland's supernatural scenes, with greenery covered magma fields and far off mountains making an ethereal scenery.

Reykjavik, the world's northernmost capital, invites you with its dynamic climate. The city's vivid design, varied road craftsmanship, and comfortable bistros add to its novel appeal. Go for a walk along the beguiling roads, visit milestones like

Hallgrímskirkja, and retain the neighborhood culture in shops and exhibitions.

Wandering past Reykjavik, Iceland's famous attractions call. The Brilliant Circle, a famous course, incorporates the geothermal marvels of Geysir and Strokkur, the noteworthy site of Thingvellir Public Park, and the strong Gullfoss cascade. Seeing the fountains emit or strolling between the structural plates at Thingvellir gives a significant association with Iceland's geographical powers.

The South Coast flaunts dark sand sea shores, emotional bluffs, and the dazzling Seljalandsfoss and Skogafoss cascades. Ice sheets like Solheimajokull offer open doors for directed ice cave investigations, adding an audacious contort to your visit.

For those looking for unwinding, the Blue Tidal pond, a geothermal spa encompassed by magma fields, is a must-visit. The smooth blue waters, plentiful in minerals, give a restoring experience against the rough Icelandic background.

Picking the Right Flight Choice: While showing up in Iceland, you have a few flight choices. Keflavik Worldwide Air terminal (KEF) is the essential global entryway. Most significant carriers offer trips to KEF, giving various decisions in light of your area and spending plan. Exploration and contrast choices with track down the best blend of accommodation and reasonableness.

Security Contemplations: Iceland is known for its high wellbeing guidelines. Keflavik Worldwide Air terminal sticks to severe security conventions. Significant transporters with strong wellbeing records frequently serve Iceland, guaranteeing a safe excursion. Really look at surveys and wellbeing evaluations for carriers to pursue an educated choice.

Exploring from the Air terminal: After arriving at KEF, transportation choices flourish. Taxis, transport transports, and vehicle rentals are promptly accessible. Taxis are helpful yet can be expensive. Transport transports offer a practical common choice, while leasing a vehicle gives adaptability. Pick in light of your inclinations and financial plan.

Booking Convenience: Choosing convenience relies upon your itinerary items. On the off chance that you have an early or late flight, consider remaining close to the air terminal. Reykjavik, the capital, is around a 45-minute drive away, offering a plenty of lodgings, inns, and guesthouses. Booking stages like Booking.com or Airbnb can assist you with finding appropriate choices in light of your inclinations and spending plan.

Lodgings Close to the Air terminal: For a fast progress from the air terminal, think about inns in the Keflavik or Reykjanesbær region. Famous decisions incorporate the Air terminal Lodging Aurora Star and the Icelandair Inn in Keflavik. These choices offer closeness to the air terminal while giving essential conveniences to an agreeable stay.

Investigating Well disposed Areas: Once settled, investigate the inviting neighborhoods of Reykjavik. The city is known for its lively culture, amicable local people, and beautiful environmental elements. Regions like the Old Harbor, Laugavegur, and Hallgrímskirkja offer a blend of noteworthy appeal and current attractions. Draw in with local people to find unlikely treasures and gain bits of knowledge into Icelandic culture.

Furthermore, you could pick a flight choice in light of your area and financial plan, focus on wellbeing, and think about transportation choices from the air terminal. While booking convenience, offset vicinity with your itinerary items, and investigate Reykjavik's accommodating neighborhoods for a credible Icelandic encounter,

Your Icelandic experience stretches out past the underlying appearance. Submerge yourself in the way of life, enjoy neighborhood luxuries, investigate regular ponders, and draw in with the cordial local people to make your visit genuinely remarkable.

Nearby Food Investigation:
Try not to pass up on the chance to enjoy Icelandic cooking. Attempt customary dishes like matured shark, sheep stew, and skyr. Reykjavik brags an assortment cafés and bistros offering both neighborhood and worldwide flavors. Adventure past the places of interest to find real Icelandic preferences.

Regular Miracles Roadtrips:
Iceland is famous for its amazing scenes. Plan roadtrips to investigate regular marvels like the Brilliant Circle, Blue Tidal pond, and Seljalandsfoss

cascade. Many visit administrators in Reykjavik offer directed outings, giving a helpful method for encountering the nation's shocking excellence.

Warm Pools and Natural aquifers:
Experience the country's geothermal marvels by visiting neighborhood pools and underground aquifers. The Blue Tidal pond is a famous decision, however consider less popular choices like the Mysterious Tidal pond or Reykjadalur Natural aquifers for a more serene encounter. Make sure to follow nearby manners while partaking in these normal showers.

Craftsmanship and Exhibition halls in Reykjavik:
Find Iceland's rich social history by investigating Reykjavik's exhibition halls and workmanship displays. The Public Gallery of Iceland, Harpa Show Corridor, and the Reykjavik Craftsmanship Exhibition hall merit a visit. Submerge yourself in Icelandic workmanship, history, and contemporary culture.

Aurora Borealis Investigation:
In the event that meeting throughout the cold weather months, it is an unquestionable requirement

to pursue Aurora Borealis. Join directed visits or adventure out all alone to get a brief look at this entrancing normal peculiarity. Settle on areas from city lights for the best review insight.

Cooperation with Local people:
Icelanders are known for their glow and kind disposition. Start up discussions with local people in bistros, shops, or during coordinated occasions. Drawing in with the local area can prompt significant bits of knowledge, proposals, and maybe new companionships.

Outside Experience Exercises:
For the experience fan, Iceland offers exercises like ice sheet climbing, ice cave investigation, and whale watching. Many visit administrators take care of various expertise levels, guaranteeing a significant and safe experience.

Celebrations and Occasions:
Check the nearby occasions schedule for celebrations and occasions occurring during your visit. Iceland has various social and live concerts consistently, furnishing an opportunity to celebrate with local people and partake in a dynamic climate.

12 PM Sun Insight:
Throughout the late spring months, Iceland encounters the peculiarity of the 12 PM Sun, where the sun sets momentarily prior to rising once more. Exploit the drawn out sunshine hours to investigate the scenes, leave on late-night climbs, or just partake in the extraordinary air during the mystical brilliant hour.

Waterfront Drives and Tourist detours:
Leasing a vehicle gives the opportunity to set out on grand drives along Iceland's pleasant shorelines. The Ring Street (Highway 1) offers an extensive excursion around the island, exhibiting different scenes, beguiling towns, and open doors for unconstrained diversions.

Interesting Shopping Finds:
Reykjavik's shopping scene is dynamic, highlighting nearby stores and markets. Investigate Laugavegur Road for style, handiworks, and gifts. Support neighborhood craftsmans and bring back home a piece of Icelandic craftsmanship, whether it's a woolen sweater, high quality ceramics, or exceptional gems.

Natural life Experiences:
Iceland's encompassing waters are wealthy in marine life. Consider taking a whale-watching visit to notice superb animals like humpback whales and orcas. Puffin states additionally speck the shore, offering birdwatching open doors, particularly in areas like Dyrhólaey and the Westman Islands.

Setting up camp and Open air Stays:
Experience Iceland's crude excellence by setting up camp in assigned regions or remaining in provincial facilities. Camping areas are exceptional, permitting you to drench yourself in nature while partaking in the solace of fundamental offices. This is a magnificent method for interfacing with Iceland's scenes on a more personal level.

Nearby Music Scene:
Investigate Reykjavik's energetic music scene, known for its variety and innovativeness. Look at neighborhood bars and settings for live exhibitions, going from conventional Icelandic music to contemporary non mainstream groups. Experience the powerful energy of the city's nightlife while partaking in the hints of Icelandic ability.

Learn Essential Icelandic Expressions:
While numerous Icelanders communicate in English, learning a couple of essential Icelandic expressions can improve your experience and recognize the nearby culture. Basic good tidings and articulations can go quite far in encouraging positive collaborations with local people.

Mindful The travel industry Practices:
Embrace mindful the travel industry by regarding the climate and neighborhood customs. Follow Leave No Follow standards while investigating regular locales, support manageable drives, and take part in exercises that advance the conservation of Iceland's special biological systems.

Chapter 6

Transportation Options in Iceland: Budgeting for Car Rental and Owning Your Own Car On Tour.

Iceland, with its shocking scenes, geothermal miracles, and remarkable social attractions, has turned into an inexorably well known objective for voyagers. Exploring this Nordic island's different territory requires an insightful thought of transportation choices. From very much kept up with streets to flighty methods of movement, Iceland offers a scope of decisions for getting around.

When owning a car in Iceland, be aware of road conditions and maintenance costs due to the challenging terrain. Budget for parking fees in popular tourist spots and plan your itinerary to minimize unnecessary driving.

Utilize public transportation or alternative modes for certain destinations to balance convenience and cost-effectiveness during your Icelandic tour. For car rentals, book in advance to secure better rates and consider compact or economy options for both cost savings and navigating narrow Icelandic roads efficiently.

When budgeting for car rental in Iceland, consider off-peak seasons for lower rates. Owning a car might be costlier due to fuel and maintenance, so weigh your options based on travel frequency and distances. Additionally, prioritize fuel-efficient vehicles to optimize expenses during your tour.

Rental Vehicles:
Iceland's street network is broad and very much kept up with, making it an ideal objective for travels. Rental vehicles, including 4x4 vehicles, are promptly accessible at the Keflavik Global Air terminal and in significant towns. This adaptability permits voyagers to investigate the notorious Ring Street, interfacing key attractions like the Brilliant Circle and the Blue Tidal pond.

Public Transports:
For those looking for a more spending plan well disposed choice, Iceland's public transport framework interfaces towns and urban communities across the island. The transport network is extensive, covering both famous traveler objections and distant

regions. Voyagers can buy transport passes for more prominent adaptability or settle on single tickets for explicit courses.

Homegrown Flights:
Iceland's tough territory can now and again make street travel tedious. Homegrown flights are accessible, connecting Reykjavik with a few territorial air terminals. This choice is especially valuable for those with restricted time who need to investigate the furthest reaches of the island, like the Westfjords or East Iceland.

Taxicabs and Ride-Sharing:
In metropolitan regions like Reykjavik, taxis are promptly accessible. Ride-sharing administrations likewise work, giving extra accommodation, particularly during the colder months while strolling may less allure. Notwithstanding, note that taxi administrations might be more restricted in country regions.

Cycling:
With its perfect air and picturesque scenes, Iceland is progressively turning into an objective for cycling devotees. Numerous streets have committed cycling paths, and daring voyagers can investigate the field on two wheels. Be that as it may, this choice requires cautious thought of weather patterns and street security.

Ships:
Iceland's beach front area implies that ships assume a part in transportation, interfacing the central area with a portion of the more modest islands. This method of movement gives an interesting point of view of Iceland's shore and can be a charming encounter for those hoping to wander outside of what might be expected.

Directed Visits:
For a calm travel insight, directed visits offer an extensive method for investigating Iceland's miracles. Whether by transport, super jeep, or even snowmobile, these visits take care of different interests, from pursuing Aurora Borealis to finding geothermal areas of interest.

Camper Vans:
Embracing the soul of experience, numerous explorers choose camper vans, transforming their excursion into a portable setting up camp insight. Various organizations offer exceptional camper vans for lease, giving both transportation and convenience. This decision considers adaptability in schedule, empowering voyagers to remain nearby nature in Iceland's amazing scenes.

Bumming a ride:
Iceland has a standing as quite possibly of the most secure nation, making catching a ride a reasonable and special choice for the more bold explorer. While it's fundamental to focus on wellbeing, numerous local people and individual voyagers participate in this public type of transportation, encouraging a feeling of fellowship and shared investigation.

Snowmobiles and ATV Visits:
In the cold weather months, when portions of Iceland are shrouded in snow, snowmobiles and off-road vehicles (ATVs) become exciting transportation choices. Visit administrators offer trips that permit guests to cross glacial masses,

volcanic scenes, and other snow-shrouded territories for an adrenaline-filled experience.

Electric Bikes:
In metropolitan regions, electric bikes have turned into a famous and eco-accommodating method for brief distance transportation. Accessible for lease through cell phone applications, these bikes offer a helpful method for investigating urban communities like Reykjavik, giving a speedy and effective method of movement while limiting ecological effect.

Horseback Riding:
For a really Icelandic encounter, consider investigating the field riding a horse. Horse riding visits take guests through dazzling scenes, giving a remarkable point of view and an association with the country's rich equestrian culture. This choice is particularly famous in areas where conventional transportation might be less down to earth.

Although, owning your own car on tour in Iceland provides the ultimate freedom to explore the breathtaking landscapes at your own pace. The rugged terrain and diverse natural wonders make Iceland a paradise for road trippers.

Choosing the Right Vehicle: Opt for a sturdy 4x4, especially if you plan to venture into the highlands or off the beaten path. Iceland's F-roads require a robust vehicle. Consider renting a camper van for added convenience, allowing you to combine transportation and accommodation.

Essential Documents: Ensure you have a valid driver's license and carry all necessary documents, including your rental agreement and insurance papers. Familiarize yourself with local driving rules and road signs.

Navigation: Use GPS navigation and offline maps, as some areas may lack network coverage. Familiarize yourself with the route beforehand to avoid confusion, and consider renting a GPS system with Icelandic maps.

Weather and Road Conditions: Iceland's weather can be unpredictable. Check road conditions regularly, especially during winter when snow and ice can impact driving. The Icelandic Road and Coastal Administration website provides real-time information on road conditions.

Camping and Accommodation: Iceland offers numerous campsites, allowing you to stay close to nature. Plan your itinerary to include these sites, and be aware of wild camping regulations. If you prefer more comfort, book accommodations in advance, especially during peak tourist seasons.

Fueling Up: Gas stations are scattered across the country, but some remote areas may have limited options. Fill up whenever you can, and consider carrying extra fuel if venturing into isolated regions.

Packing Essentials: Pack warm clothing, waterproof gear, and sturdy footwear. Iceland's weather can change rapidly, and you'll want to be prepared for all conditions. Don't forget your camera to capture the stunning landscapes.

Hot Springs and Attractions: Discover Iceland's unique attractions, including hot springs like the Blue Lagoon and hidden gems like the Secret

Lagoon. Plan your route to include these stops for a relaxing break amidst nature.

Safety Tips: Inform someone about your travel plans, especially if heading into more remote areas. Be cautious of wildlife on the roads, and respect local regulations to ensure a safe and enjoyable journey.

Cultural Etiquette: Respect the environment and local communities. Stay on designated paths, avoid disturbing wildlife, and follow the 'leave no trace' principle to preserve Iceland's pristine nature

All in all, while considering transportation choices for visits in Iceland, it's significant to gauge the benefits and burdens of leasing a vehicle as opposed to using coordinated visits. Leasing a vehicle gives unrivaled adaptability, permitting voyagers to investigate at their own speed and find off in an unexpected direction areas. Be that as it may, it accompanies liabilities like route, powering, and possible weather conditions difficulties.

Then again, coordinated visits offer comfort and nearby mastery, guaranteeing a problem free encounter. This is especially advantageous in Iceland, where capricious atmospheric conditions and testing territories can present obstructions to autonomous voyagers. Be that as it may, these visits might restrict adaptability and customized investigation.

Possessing a vehicle in Iceland for visits is by and large unfeasible for guests because of the related expenses and operations. Vehicle rentals stay the most famous decision, finding some kind of harmony among opportunity and comfort. At last, the decision between leasing a vehicle and joining coordinated visits relies upon individual inclinations, travel style, and the ideal degree of control and direction during the Icelandic experience.

Chapter 7

The Rules Instructions on Iceland Laws and Ethics for Visitors.

Iceland, with its amazing scenes and dynamic culture, invites guests from around the globe. To guarantee an amicable encounter for the two travelers and local people, it is pivotal for guests to really get to know the regulations and morals that oversee this Nordic island country. Regarding these rules improves the explorer's visit as well as adds to the protection of Iceland's exceptional climate and cultural qualities.

a. Lawful System

Natural Stewardship: Iceland flaunts unblemished normal magnificence, and guests should comply to severe natural guidelines. Keeping away from rough terrain driving, remaining on assigned ways, and regarding untamed life territories are central. The Icelandic government puts a high need on safeguarding its immaculate scenes, and sightseers assume a fundamental part in keeping up with this fragile equilibrium.

Traffic Rules: Icelandic streets, however frequently uncrowded, request cautious route. Guests ought to know about speed limits, street signs, and the significance of headlights, in any event, during light hours. The country's assorted atmospheric conditions require additional watchfulness, particularly in winter when cold streets represent extra difficulties.

Liquor and Tobacco Regulations: The lawful savoring age Iceland is 20, and liquor is sold exclusively in state-run stores known as "Vínbúðin." Vacationers ought to find out more about these guidelines to guarantee consistence. Smoking is precluded in encased public spaces, underlining Iceland's obligation to general wellbeing and prosperity.

b. Social Morals

Regard for Security: Icelanders exceptionally esteem their security. Guests ought to be aware of individual space and stay away from meddling way of behaving. Looking for consent prior to taking photos of people is a typical kindness, reflecting admiration for the nearby culture.

Resistance and Inclusivity: Iceland is known for its receptive and comprehensive society. Guests ought to embrace this soul and recognize variety. Segregation in light of race, orientation, or sexual direction conflicts with the center standards of Icelandic morals.

Geothermal Manners: The country's geothermal marvels are a significant fascination, however washing decorum should be noticed. Showering prior to entering underground aquifers or pools is obligatory, guaranteeing tidiness and cleanliness. This training additionally mirrors the Icelandic accentuation on public obligation.

c. Social Obligation

Squander The board: Iceland puts areas of strength for an on capable garbage removal. Guests ought to use assigned containers for reusing and general waste, adding to the country's obligation to natural manageability.

Untamed life Cooperation: While experiencing untamed life is a completely exhilarating part of visiting Iceland, noticing creatures from a protected distance is fundamental. Upsetting or taking care of untamed life is completely deterred to keep up with the normal ways of behaving of these species.

Nearby Economy Backing: Adding to the nearby economy is empowered. Settling on privately created labor and products cultivates monetary manageability and supports the jobs of Icelanders. Guests ought to investigate the rich cluster of Icelandic items, from handiworks to customary cooking.

d. Security Conventions

Climate Readiness: Iceland's weather conditions can be erratic, with abrupt changes and testing conditions. Guests ought to remain informed about weather conditions figures, particularly if wandering into far off regions. Appropriate attire and hardware are fundamental for outside exercises to guarantee wellbeing and happiness.

Crisis Administrations: Looking into crisis contact numbers and the area of the closest medical care offices is vital. Iceland puts a high need on security, and speedy admittance to help can be crucial if there should be an occurrence of unanticipated occasions.

e. Social Legacy Safeguarding

Verifiable Locales and Antiques: Iceland is wealthy in verifiable locales and antiques. Guests ought to abstain from contacting or upsetting these social fortunes. Regarding the uprightness of authentic locales guarantees that people in the future can likewise see the value in the country's legacy.

Language Graciousness: While English is broadly spoken, learning a couple of fundamental Icelandic expressions exhibits a real interest in the nearby culture. Islanders value guests really trying to impart in their language, cultivating positive cooperations.

f. Convenience Rules

Setting up camp Guidelines: Setting up camp is a famous method for encountering Iceland's outside.

Nonetheless, it should be done dependably. Wild setting up camp is precluded in numerous areas, and campers ought to utilize assigned camping areas with appropriate offices to limit ecological effect.

Inns and Guesthouses: While remaining in facilities, guests ought to know about house rules and guidelines. Regarding calm hours and keeping explicit rules set by the foundation adds to an amicable concurrence with different visitors and the neighborhood local area.

g. Alerts With respect to Untamed life

Bird Settling Regions: Certain regions in Iceland act as settling justification for seabirds. Guests are encouraged to be careful in these zones, regarding limited admittance regions during reproducing seasons to stay away from aggravation to the avian populace.

Horse Communication: Icelandic ponies are a one of a kind variety, and connections ought to be drawn closer with care. Taking care of them without authorization or participating in problematic way of behaving can trouble these creatures. Keeping rules given by horse-riding visits guarantees a positive encounter for the two guests and the ponies.

h. Municipal Commitment

Public Showings: Icelanders effectively partake in municipal issues. On the off chance that guests experience public shows or social events, it is fitting to see from a conscious distance. Monitoring the nearby setting and exhibiting social responsiveness adds to a serene conjunction.

Local area Commitment: Partaking in neighborhood occasions and merriments is empowered. This cultivates a feeling of local area and permits guests to acquire further experiences into Icelandic practices and lifestyles. Deferential support in far-reaching developments enhances the general travel insight.

i. The Travel industry Rules

Cold Investigation: Iceland's ice sheets are dazzling, however wandering onto them requires alert. Guests participating in ice sheet related exercises ought to do as such with authorized guides, as they have the vital ability to securely explore these powerful conditions.

Volcanic Regions: Investigation of volcanic locales is a special encounter, however it ought to be drawn nearer with care. Following assigned ways and regarding wellbeing admonitions is significant, taking into account the potential dangers related with volcanic scenes.

j. Aurora Borealis Manners

Regard for Obscurity: Aurora Borealis, or Aurora Borealis, are a heavenly exhibition frequently noticeable in Iceland. To improve the experience for all, guests ought to limit light contamination by switching out pointless lights, permitting everybody to partake in the regular miracle in its full brightness.

Photography Contemplations: Catching Aurora Borealis is a shared objective for guests. Utilizing photography hardware dependably, for example, keeping away from meddlesome blazes and limiting unsettling influences, guarantees a common delight in this divine peculiarity.

k. International Contemplations

Line Guidelines: Guests ought to remain informed about line guidelines, remembering visa necessities and any new changes for movement approaches. Following these guidelines guarantees a smooth section and leave process, adding to a positive generally travel insight.

Regard for Native Culture: Collaboration with Iceland's native populace, especially the Sami public, ought to be drawn closer with social responsiveness. Regarding their customs and land privileges cultivates shared understanding and appreciation.

l. Wellbeing and Health Practices

Underground aquifers Cleanliness: Partaking in Iceland's natural aquifers is a well known movement, yet it is urgent to keep up with individual cleanliness. Guests ought to shower completely prior to entering common underground aquifers to maintain neatness guidelines and advance a charming encounter for all.

Clinical benefits Mindfulness: Finding out more about the area of clinical offices and it is essential to comprehend medical care administrations. While Iceland gives top notch clinical consideration, being ready for potential medical problems guarantees a calm visit.

m. Monetary Obligation

Money and Installment Techniques: Figuring out Iceland's cash (ISK) and its worth is fundamental for monetary exchanges. While Mastercards are broadly acknowledged, having some neighborhood money available can be valuable, particularly in additional far off regions.

Tipping Customs: Tipping is certainly not a typical practice in Iceland, as administration charges are frequently included. In any case, gathering together the bill or offering thanks verbally is valued.

In synopsis, a complete comprehension of Iceland's regulations and morals improves the guest experience across a range of exercises — from bold pursuits to social commitment. By embracing these rules, explorers add to the conservation of Iceland's normal marvels, maintain social regard, and guarantee a positive effect on both the climate and neighborhood networks.

Understanding and complying with Iceland's regulations and morals isn't just a lawful commitment yet in addition a significant articulation of regard for the nation's legacy and values. By embracing these rules, guests become dynamic members in safeguarding Iceland's regular marvels and social honesty. At last, a careful and kind way to deal with investigation guarantees a positive and improving experience for all who have the honor of finding this dazzling country. it is a pledge to capable the travel industry and social appreciation. By incorporating these rules into their movement conduct, guests add to the supportability of Iceland's regular marvels, social legacy, and local area prosperity. This aggregate exertion guarantees that the magnificence and uniqueness of Iceland persevere for a long time into the future.

Chapter 8

Iceland Cultural Events
and Festivals

Iceland, with its shocking scenes and energetic culture, has a plenty of interesting widespread developments and celebrations over time. These festivals offer a profound plunge into the country's rich legacy, mixing customary Icelandic traditions with contemporary imaginative articulations. From live concerts like Iceland Wireless transmissions to the captivating Winter Lights Celebration, every occasion gives a brief look into the nation's creative, scholarly, and culinary fortunes. As we investigate Iceland's social embroidery, we'll dig into the meaning of these celebrations and how they add to the island's feeling of local area and personality.

Iceland's social schedule is accentuated with occasions that exhibit the versatility and innovativeness of its kin. The Þorrablót, a colder time of year celebration established in old Norse customs, is a culinary experience where local people enjoy customary Icelandic dishes, supporting the connection between the over a significant time span.

Conversely, the Reykjavik Expressions Celebration changes the capital into a center of imaginative investigation, including a different scope of exhibitions, shows, and establishments that feature the country's contemporary social scene.

The Mysterious Solstice Celebration, held throughout the late spring solstice, is a music event that draws worldwide craftsmen and music devotees to the place where there is fire and ice. Against the setting of Iceland's strange scenes, participants revel in the soul of this special celebration, making recollections that reverberate long after the music blurs.

Writing holds a unique spot in Iceland's social legacy, and the Reykjavik Worldwide Scholarly Celebration is a demonstration of the country's abstract ability. Famous writers, artists, and masterminds unite to examine and praise the composed word, encouraging an affection for writing that rises above borders.

The Icelandic Public Day on June seventeenth denotes the country's autonomy from Denmark, uniting networks for marches, shows, and customary merriments. It's daily of public pride and solidarity, highlighting's areas of strength for Iceland of personality. Iceland's far-reaching developments and celebrations grandstand the country's rich legacy and dynamic imaginative scene. The schedule is specked with festivities that mirror the island's set of experiences, old stories, and contemporary inventiveness.

Þorrablót: This midwinter celebration, generally held in January and February, celebrates customary Icelandic food. Members enjoy exceptional dishes like hákarl (aged shark) and sviðasulta (head cheddar).

Freedom Day: June seventeenth denotes the day when Iceland acquired autonomy from Denmark in 1944. Merriments incorporate motorcades, shows, and a vivacious air all through the country.

Reykjavik Expressions Celebration: This conspicuous occasion, held yearly in May, features different fine arts like music, theater, dance, and visual expressions. Worldwide and neighborhood craftsmen add to the city's social dynamic quality.

Iceland Wireless transmissions: A prestigious live concert occurring in November, Iceland Wireless transmissions draws in both nearby and worldwide demonstrations. Reykjavik changes into a melodic center, highlighting exhibitions in different classifications.

Verslunarmannahelgi: Interpreted as "Work Day Weekend," this August celebration joins open air exercises with music and widespread developments. Families frequently go setting up camp, and the environment is loaded up with merriments.

Culture Night (Menningarnótt): Held in August, this occasion transforms Reykjavik into a monstrous outside festival. The roads wake up with music, workmanship establishments, and different exhibitions, offering a sample of Iceland's inventive soul.

Secret Solstice: Known for its remarkable setting throughout the mid year solstice, this live concert in June flaunts exhibitions in an extraordinary area, supplemented by the mysterious Icelandic summer sunshine.

The Public Day: Celebrated on June seventeenth, Public Day incorporates marches, shows, and different widespread developments. It's an energetic festival with a solid feeling of local area soul.

Christmas in Iceland: The Christmas season is a mysterious time in Iceland. Conventional Yule Chaps, legends figures, and merry business sectors make a colder time of year wonderland climate, making Christmas a treasured social festival.

Háskarinn: This film celebration in Reykjavik centers around exhibiting Icelandic and global film. It gives a stage to movie producers to share their novel points of view.

Icelandic Writing Days: A festival of Iceland's rich scholarly legacy, this occasion regularly happens in April. It incorporates readings, book dispatches, and conversations, underscoring the significance of writing in Icelandic culture.

Reykjavik Style Celebration: Displaying both Icelandic and worldwide originators, this yearly occasion in Spring puts a focus on the developing design scene in Iceland, mixing Nordic feel with worldwide patterns.

Solfar Sun Explorer Show Series: Held throughout the late spring months, this show series exploits the lengthy light hours, offering open air exhibitions at the famous Sun Explorer design in Reykjavik.

Icelandic People Live concert: Praising the rural's music customs, this celebration assembles artists and fans to investigate and value the foundations of Icelandic melodic culture.

Aurora Borealis Celebration: Exploiting Iceland's shocking normal peculiarity, this colder time of year celebration consolidates music, expressions, and culture under the moving auroras, making an extraordinary and charming experience.

Eistnaflug: Known as Iceland's greatest metal celebration, Eistnaflug draws in both Icelandic and global metal groups and fans. It's a high-energy occasion held in the town of Neskaupstaður.

Icelandic Adventure Week: Praising the adventures that are necessary to Icelandic writing, this occasion in June incorporates talks, shows, and exhibitions, offering experiences into the country's authentic accounts.

DesignMarch: Exhibiting the best in Icelandic plan, this celebration in Spring unites originators, specialists, and trailblazers to show their work in different imaginative fields, from style to engineering.

Icelandic Climbing Celebration: Embracing the nation's dazzling scenes, this celebration in July urges open air fans to investigate Iceland's different landscape through coordinated climbs and nature-related exercises.

Celebration of the Ocean: Observing Iceland's sea legacy, this occasion in August incorporates boat races, ocean related rivalries, and merriments along the coast, featuring the significance of the sea to Icelandic culture and history.

All in all, Iceland's far-reaching developments and celebrations assume a critical part in saving and commending the rich legacy of this Nordic country.

These dynamic events exhibit Iceland's creative gifts as well as encourage a feeling of local area and public personality. From the notorious Reykjavik Expressions Celebration to the remarkable Þorrablót winter celebration, every occasion adds to the social woven artwork of the country.

Moreover, these celebrations act as stages for both conventional and contemporary articulations of Icelandic personality. The combination of old stories with present day creative undertakings mirrors the powerful idea of Icelandic culture, featuring its capacity to develop while remaining established in custom. This combination is especially clear in occasions like the Icelandic Public Day festivities, where the country remembers its freedom with a mix of verifiable reflections and contemporary celebrations.

Chapter 9

Accommodation Options in Iceland:
Budgeting for Rental Home and Hotels.

Iceland offers a different scope of convenience choices, taking special care of different inclinations and spending plans. From comfortable guesthouses to lavish inns, guests can track down reasonable lodgings the nation over. Reykjavik, the capital, flaunts various inns, lodgings, and store facilities, giving simple admittance to the city's energetic culture. For those looking for a more vivid encounter, rustic regions offer beguiling guesthouses and ranch stays, permitting visitors to interface with Iceland's regular magnificence.

Camping areas are famous throughout the mid year, giving a reasonable and gutsy method for encountering the shocking scenes. Furthermore, novel choices like resting cases and ice lodgings offer particular stays. The convenience foundation in Iceland has extended lately, guaranteeing that explorers can find agreeable lodgings no matter what their inclinations, making the country an enticing objective for a large number of guests.

Arranging a visit to the pleasant scenes of Iceland includes wondering about its shocking regular magnificence as well as guaranteeing an agreeable and reasonable stay. Whether you're thinking about a rental home or an inn, making a thoroughly examined financial plan is urgent for a consistent and pleasant experience. Iceland, known for its novel mix of ice sheets, volcanoes, and natural aquifers, offers an assortment of convenience choices, each with its own expense contemplations. In this aide, we will dive into the fundamentals of planning for rental homes and lodgings in Iceland, assisting you with finding some kind of harmony among solace and monetary reasonability during your Icelandic experience.

Understanding the Icelandic Convenience Scene:

Prior to plunging into planning particulars, getting a handle on the variety of convenience decisions in Iceland is fundamental. From comfortable houses concealed in remote scenes to present day lodgings in clamoring downtown areas, the choices are essentially as differed as the nation's scenes. This variety permits explorers to fit their visit to their inclinations, whether that includes submerging themselves in the peacefulness of nature or partaking in the accommodations of metropolitan living.

Convenience Choices in Iceland: An Exhaustive Aide
Iceland, known for its staggering scenes and novel normal marvels, offers an assortment of convenience choices to suit various inclinations and financial plans. Whether you're searching for a comfortable home stay or an extravagant lodging, Iceland has something for everybody.

a. Inns

Lavish Lodgings: Iceland brags a reach upscale inns, particularly in Reykjavik. These inns offer first rate conveniences, spa offices, and stunning perspectives. Models incorporate the Particle Experience Inn and the Retreat at Blue Tidal pond.
Spending plan Cordial Lodgings: For a more efficient stay, consider financial plan well disposed inns like Fosshotel or CenterHotel in Reykjavik.

These choices give agreeable facilities without burning through every last cent.

b. Guesthouses

Beguiling Homestays: Guesthouses give a more personal encounter, frequently run by local people. They offer an opportunity to interface with the way of life and are dissipated all through the country. Places like Heimaey Guesthouse in Vestmannaeyjar exhibit Icelandic accommodation.

c. Excursion Rentals

Airbnbs and Occasion Homes: Leasing a confidential home or condo through stages like Airbnb considers a warm encounter. An extraordinary choice for those incline toward more freedom and security. Costs change contingent upon area, size, and conveniences.

d. Lodgings

Spending plan Cordial Dormitories: Lodgings are well known among financial plan explorers and solo swashbucklers. Reykjavik has a few lodgings, similar to Space Inn, offering dorm style convenience with shared offices. Lodgings are an extraordinary cash saving tip and meet individual explorers.

e. Ranch Stays

Provincial Retreats: For a novel encounter, consider remaining at a homestead. Iceland offers ranch stays where you can submerge yourself in country life. These facilities frequently give a comfortable environment and an opportunity to encounter neighborhood customs.

Planning Tips

Off-Pinnacle Travel: Consider visiting during the shoulder seasons (spring or tumble) to find lower convenience costs and less groups.

Book Ahead of time: Getting your convenience early can assist you with catching more ideal arrangements, particularly during top vacationer seasons.

Furthermore, planning for facilities in Iceland is a vital part of outing arranging, taking into account the nation's one of a kind and spellbinding scenes. Whether you're picking rentals, inns, or home stays, a thoroughly examined financial plan guarantees an agreeable and charming stay while investigating the miracles of this Nordic island.

Iceland, eminent for its staggering regular excellence, is an objective that draws in explorers looking for experience and unwinding the same. To capitalize on your visit, it's fundamental to comprehend the assorted convenience choices accessible and how to actually financial plan.

Rentals:
Iceland offers a scope of rental facilities, from comfortable houses to smart lofts. Planning for rentals includes considering variables like area, size, and conveniences. Costs can change contingent upon whether you're remaining in the capital city, Reykjavik, or investigating the more far off areas. It's prudent to research and book rentals ahead of time, particularly during top traveler seasons, to get ideal rates.

Inns:

The lodging scene in Iceland takes care of different inclinations, from extravagance foundations to more spending plan well disposed choices. While planning for inns, consider the star rating, area, and included administrations. While lodgings in Reykjavik might be pricier, investigating choices in more modest towns or rustic regions can offer financially savvy options. Moreover, reserving adaptable rates and watching out for advancements can add to investment funds.

Home Stays:

Home stays, frequently worked with through stages like Airbnb, give an extraordinary chance to encounter Icelandic culture firsthand. Planning for home stays includes thinking about the length of stay, conveniences, and host audits. This convenience choice is in many cases more conservative for longer visits, as it permits you to save money on eating costs by setting up your feasts. Drawing in with local people can likewise upgrade your general travel insight.

In outline, planning for rentals, lodgings, and home stays in Iceland requires a smart methodology, considering factors like area, span of stay, and individual inclinations. Investigating choices well ahead of time, investigating different region of the nation, and being adaptable with your movement dates can add to a more practical and charming stay in this captivating objective.

Chapter 10

Best Time to Visit Iceland for Perfect Weather And Memorable Experiences.

Iceland's weather conditions differs over time, offering interesting encounters for guests. The best chance to visit generally relies upon your inclinations and the exercises you have as a primary concern.

Summer (June-August):
This period flaunts the mildest temperatures, going from 10°C to 20°C (50°F to 68°F). Summer gives long sunshine hours, taking into consideration broadened investigation of Iceland's shocking scenes, cascades, and springs. The energetic vegetation and blossoming wildflowers improve the pleasant view. It's an optimal time for climbing, setting up camp, and travels.

Pre-summer (May) and Early Harvest time (September):

These momentary months offer a harmony between reasonable temperatures and less groups. The scene is as yet rich, and the days are sensibly lengthy, making it an extraordinary time for open air exercises. Also, you could get Aurora Borealis in September as the evenings obscure.

Late Fall (October-November) and Late-winter (Walk April):
While temperatures decrease during these months, they carry the valuable chance to observe the entrancing Aurora Borealis. The colder environment likewise implies less travelers, taking into consideration a more quiet encounter. Remember that a few good country streets may be shut down, restricting openness to specific regions.

Winter (December-February):
Winter in Iceland offers a remarkable appeal, with snow-covered scenes and the chance of seeing Aurora Borealis at their pinnacle. In any case, temperatures can decrease fundamentally, going from - 10°C to 5°C (14°F to 41°F). Winter sports fans can

appreciate exercises like ice buckling and skiing.

On the off chance that you're an open air aficionado and wish to investigate Iceland's different greenery, summer is the ideal time. The wide open wakes up with beautiful wildflowers, and transient birds run to the island, making a birdwatcher's heaven. The well known climbing trails, for example, the Laugavegur Trail, are more available during these months.

In the event that you're a photography lover, the delicate tints of the 12 PM sun in summer or the distinct difference of the cold scenes against Aurora Borealis in winter give unbelievable open doors. Catch notorious sights like the Jokulsarlon Icy mass Tidal pond, the dark sand sea shores of Vik, or the extraordinary scenes of Landmannalaugar.

In the event that you seriously love marine life, visiting Iceland in the mid year gives an astounding an open door to whale watching. The waterfront regions become focal points for different whale species, including minke, humpback, and, surprisingly, the subtle blue whale. Take a boat visit from places like Husavik or Reykjavik for an opportunity to observe these magnificent animals right at home.

Experience searchers can exploit the lengthy sunshine hours in summer for exciting exercises like glacial mass climbing, ice climbing, or in any event, investigating ice caves. Vatnajokull Public Park, Europe's biggest public park, offers a dazzling setting for such experiences.

On the off chance that you're keen on the neighborhood culture and history, going to the yearly Icelandic Public Day on June seventeenth is an extraordinary method for drenching yourself in the nation's practices. Marches, shows, and different occasions occur the nation over to observe Iceland's autonomy.

For those looking for a more separated and tranquil experience, the shoulder seasons give a calmer climate. Spring carries the enlivening of nature with softening snow and arising untamed life, while fall grandstands Iceland's scenes embellished in brilliant tones. During these momentary periods, you'll experience less travelers, taking into consideration a more cozy association with the environmental factors.

Remember that the climate in Iceland can be capricious whenever of the year, so come ready with layers, waterproof apparel, and strong footwear. Moreover, consider leasing a vehicle to freely investigate the country's distant regions.

Despite when you visit, make certain to enjoy Iceland's remarkable social encounters. Visit the capital, Reykjavik, to investigate its dynamic expressions scene, appreciate nearby cooking, and loosen up in geothermal pools like the Blue Tidal pond. Regardless of the time, Iceland offers an abundance of regular marvels and social jewels for an extraordinary excursion.

Consider timing your visit to match with unique occasions like the Mysterious Solstice Celebration in June, where you can appreciate music exhibitions under the constant sunshine. On the other hand, encountering the Icelandic Christmas customs in December adds a happy touch to your excursion.

For a special experience, investigate the good countries throughout the late spring months when the inside streets are open. This tough territory offers an alternate point of view of Iceland, with its volcanic scenes, underground aquifers, and immaculate wild.

Recollect that convenience and famous attractions can book up rapidly during top seasons, so plan and book ahead of time for a smoother and more charming outing. Whether you're pursuing cascades, wondering about ice sheets, or looking for social drenching, Iceland's different contributions take care of different interests consistently.

In conclusion, for a loosening up encounter, visit the geothermal pools and natural aquifers dispersed all through the country. While the Blue Tidal pond is popular, consider searching out calmer and more regular natural aquifers for a tranquil and restoring splash.

In outline, the best opportunity to visit Iceland relies upon your inclinations and interests, yet with its different contributions, Iceland guarantees a vital encounter paying little mind to when you decide to investigate this

Picking Exercises In view of Seasons:

Summer Experiences (June-August):

- 12 PM sun takes into consideration broadened investigation.
- Ideal for setting up camp, climbing, and getting a charge out of open air celebrations.
- Natural life lovers can recognize puffins and seals along the coasts.

- Go to the Reykjavik Expressions Celebration displaying neighborhood and global specialists.
- Experience the vivacious environment of the Mysterious Solstice live concert in June.

Pre-winter Persona (September-October):

- Witness the stupendous fall foliage as the scene changes.
- Experience the novel mix of fall tones and Aurora Borealis.
- Take part in neighborhood reap celebrations exhibiting Icelandic culture.
- Participate in the Icelandic Writing Month festivities with book-related occasions.
- Go to the Reykjavik Worldwide Film Celebration for a social encounter.

Winter Sorcery (December-February):

- Embrace the colder time of year wonderland with snow-covered scenes.
- Ideal time for aurora hunting, particularly in distant areas.
- Take part in winter sports like skiing, snowmobiling, and ice climbing.
- Embrace the occasion soul at Christmas markets in Reykjavik.
- Take part in Þorrablót, a customary Icelandic midwinter celebration.

Spring Arousing (Walk April):

- Witness the progressive return of lively varieties as snow softens.
- Partake in the sight and sound of strong cascades at their pinnacle.
- Experience a calmer climate before the traveler season gets.
- Taking into account Groups and Facilities:
- Praise the appearance of spring at the Reykjavik Society Celebration.

- Participate in the merriments of the Reykjavik Dance Celebration in April.

Summer Pinnacle (June-August):

- High vacationer season with additional groups.
- Facilities and visits might require advance booking.
- Investigate beach front regions to recognize puffins, seals, and different seabirds.
- Join whale-watching visits so that an opportunity could see orcas and humpback whales.

Summer:

- Pack layers for variable climate.
- Plan exercises around the lengthy sunlight hours.

Harvest time:

- Bring waterproof stuff for infrequent downpour.

- Be ready for more limited sunlight hours.

Winter:

- Dress comfortably in protected, waterproof apparel.
- Check street conditions and terminations for winter travel.

Spring:

- Pack for both winter and momentary climate.
- Embrace the powerful scenes as nature stirs.

Chapter 11

Iceland Top Tourist Destinations You Must See.

Iceland, a place that is known for charming scenes and G miracles, remains as an enthralling objective for explorers looking for one of a kind encounters. From flowing cascades and geothermal wonders to glacial masses and dynamic urban communities, Iceland brags different cluster attractions that make it a must-visit for any swashbuckler.

Reykjavik - The Energetic Capital
Start off your Icelandic process in Reykjavik, the nation's capital and the world's northernmost capital city. This enchanting center consolidates innovation with a profound feeling of custom, offering guests a mix of contemporary workmanship, exuberant music scenes, and notable destinations like the notorious Hallgrímskirkja church.

The Brilliant Circle - Nature's Set of three
Leave on the prestigious Brilliant Circle highway, an entrancing circuit that includes three outstanding regular marvels. Look in wonder at the strong Gullfoss cascade, witness the emitting fountains at

Geysir Geothermal Region, and wonder about the structural plates meeting at Thingvellir Public Park, an UNESCO World Legacy Site.

The Blue Tidal pond - Geothermal Joy
Enjoy the supernatural experience of the Blue Tidal pond, a geothermal spa set in the midst of a magma field. The smooth blue, mineral-rich waters give a loosening up evade, offering an extraordinary juxtaposition to the rough Icelandic territory. Loosen up in the warm waters while encompassed by shocking volcanic scenes.

Jökulsárlón Glacial mass Tidal pond - Frosty Loftiness
Adventure southeast to observe the ethereal excellence of Jökulsárlón Icy mass Tidal pond. Wonder about seeing ice shelves drifting nimbly on the tidal pond, starting from the Vatnajökull Glacial mass. The differentiating shades of blue and white make a beautiful scene, making it a picture taker's heaven.

Skógafoss and Seljalandsfoss Cascades - Nature's Ensemble

Iceland's cascades are absolutely stunning, and Skógafoss and Seljalandsfoss embody this excellence. Feel the fog all over as you feel overwhelmed by the strong fountains, encompassed by rich green scenes. Seljalandsfoss even permits daring spirits to stroll in the background of water.

Vik - Dark Sand Ocean side and Basalt Segments

Visit the beguiling town of Vik, home to the famous Reynisfjara Dark Sand Ocean side. Appreciate the emotional basalt segments ascending from the ocean and the Reynisdrangar ocean stacks seaward. The glaring difference between the dull sand, thundering waves, and the encompassing bluffs causes a situation straight out of a dream.

Akureyri - The Capital of the North

Find the social and verifiable extravagance of Akureyri, Iceland's second-biggest city, settled in the beautiful Eyjafjörður fjord. Investigate the beguiling roads, visit the professional flowerbeds, and experience the energetic expressions scene that characterizes this northern pearl.

Snæfellsnes Landmass - Supernatural Scenes
Dig into the mysterious scenes of the Snæfellsnes
Promontory, frequently alluded to as "Iceland in
Smaller than expected." This far off locale
epitomizes a different exhibit of regular marvels,
from the notorious Snæfellsjökull well of lava to the
rough precipices of Arnarstapi. The region is
saturated with old stories, trusted by some to be a
wellspring of enchanted energy.

Húsavík - Whale Watching Capital
For nature fans, Húsavík allures as the
whale-watching capital of Iceland. Set out on an
oceanic experience in Skjálfandi Narrows, where
you can experience great whales, dolphins, and
seabirds. The actual town oozes enchant, with
brilliant houses coating the harbor and a sea
exhibition hall observing Iceland's nautical history.

Landmannalaugar - Good country Desert garden
Adventure into the distant good countries to find
Landmannalaugar, a geothermal desert spring
encompassed by energetic rhyolite mountains. The
dreamlike scene is dabbed with natural aquifers,

offering brave climbers an opportunity to investigate the powerful territory on bright paths. Landmannalaugar is a shelter for those looking for both isolation and a one of a kind geothermal encounter.

Westfjords - Immaculate Wild
For an off in an unexpected direction experience, investigate the remote and wild scenes of the Westfjords. Emotional fjords, steep bluffs, and interesting fishing towns portray this detached district. The disconnection of the Westfjords gives a true look into Iceland's untamed wild, making it a safe house for nature sweethearts and experience searchers.

Ásbyrgi Gulch - Horseshoe-formed Wonder
Drench yourself in the land miracles of Ásbyrgi, a horseshoe-molded gully with transcending precipices. Legends propose it was shaped by the hoofprint of Odin's eight-legged pony. The lavish forest inside the gorge offers an unmistakable difference to Iceland's ordinary scenes, giving a tranquil retreat to consideration and investigation.

THekla Fountain of liquid magma - Passage to the Hidden world

Find the folklore encompassing Hekla, Iceland's most well known fountain of liquid magma frequently connected with fables about witches and heavenly creatures. Hekla's distinct magnificence and verifiable importance make it a convincing objective for those captivated by the convergence of geography and Icelandic adventures.

Þórsmörk - Valley of Thor

Settled among icy masses and encompassed by rough mountains, Þórsmörk, or the Valley of Thor, offers a shelter for climbers and nature devotees. Open by unique transports or 4x4 vehicles, this far off valley gives a wild encounter different scenes, waterway intersections, and all encompassing perspectives on ice sheets like Eyjafjallajökull.

Snæfellsjökull Public Park - Entryway to the Focal point of the Earth

Investigate the enamoring Snæfellsjökull Public Park, known for its notable glacial mass covered well of lava. Trusted by some to be an entry to the focal point of the Earth, this enchanted region propelled Jules Verne's "Excursion to the Focal point of the Earth." The recreation area envelops different biological systems, from waterfront precipices to magma fields, making it a microcosm of Iceland's regular miracles.

Icelandic Good countries - Tough and Remote
For the bold voyager, the Icelandic Good countries entice with their crude, untamed magnificence. Remote and testing to get to, this immense wild flaunts volcanic deserts, steaming underground aquifers, and dreamlike scenes. The Laugavegur and Fimmvörðuháls climbing trails offer a vivid excursion through this rough territory.

Glymur - Iceland's Tallest Cascade
Leave on a climbing experience to observe Glymur, Iceland's tallest cascade. Concealed in Hvalfjörður fjord, the path prompting Glymur gives a visual banquet of flowing water as well as all encompassing perspectives on the encompassing fjord. The excursion to Glymur adds a component of experience, crossing a stream and navigating grand scenes.

Grímsey Island - Cold Circle Crossing
For a special geological encounter, dare to Grímsey
Island, which rides the Icy Circle. Open by ship or
little plane, this far off island offers an opportunity
to cross into the Cold Circle, set apart by a painted
line. The island's quietness, birdlife, and Cold Circle
imagery make it a particular objective.

Aurora Borealis - Aurora Borealis Scene
Iceland's colder time of year evenings wake up with
the hypnotizing dance of Aurora Borealis. Go to
distant areas from city lights, like Thingvellir Public
Park or the Jökulsárlón Glacial mass Tidal pond, for
an opportunity to observe the ethereal shine of the
Aurora Borealis painting the night sky.

All in all, Iceland's top traveler objections offer a
mix of normal marvels, social encounters, and
geothermal enjoyments. Whether you're enraptured
by the lively city life in Reykjavik, the land wonders
along the Brilliant Circle, or the tranquil
magnificence of ice sheets and cascades, Iceland
guarantees a remarkable excursion for each traveler.

Chapter 12

Dining and entertainment restaurants in Iceland.

Feasting and diversion in Iceland offer a novel mix of neighborhood flavors and social encounters. Reykjavik, the capital, is a center for different feasting choices. Customary Icelandic cooking, for example, hákarl (aged shark) and sheep dishes, can be enjoyed at eateries like Þrír Frakkar. For a cutting edge curve, foundations like Dill center around Nordic fixings with a contemporary energy.

The culinary scene stretches out past Reykjavik, with beguiling bistros in unassuming communities and towns serving custom made treats. Also, fish devotees can savor the catch of the day at seaside diners like Fjöruborðið in Stokkseyri.

Diversion frequently includes a mix of food, music, and Icelandic old stories. Scenes like Harpa Show Corridor have different exhibitions, while themed eateries like The Viking Town give vivid encounters, complete with conventional music and narrating.

During summer, the 12 PM Sun gives a charming setting to in the open air feasting. In the interim, winter offers an opportunity to observe Aurora Borealis, for certain cafés integrating this divine presentation into their climate.

a. Customary Icelandic Food:

Þrír Frakkar (Three Coats): Settled in Reykjavik, Þrír Frakkar is a shelter for those looking for a valid taste of Icelandic cooking. Test aged shark (Hákarl), sheep dishes, and conventional fish stews ready with privately obtained fixings.

Matur og Drykkur (Food and Drink): Situated in a noteworthy area of Reykjavik, Matur og Drykkur offers a cutting edge curve to conventional dishes. Amuse your taste buds with their creative interpretation of exemplary Icelandic flavors, like smoked puffin and sheep.

b. Fish Party:

Sjávarkjallarinn (The Fish Basement): Arranged in Reykjavik, Sjávarkjallarinn is a fish darling's heaven. Enjoy different new gets, including langoustines, salmon, and cod, skillfully ready to feature the immaculateness of Icelandic waters.

Humarhúsið (The Lobster House): Found in the core of Reykjavik's harbor, Humarhúsið is eminent for its lobster-driven menu. Appreciate lobster bisque, barbecued lobster tails, and other perfect dishes highlighting this valued Icelandic fish.

c. Global Combination:

Dill: Granted a Michelin star, Dill in Reykjavik consistently mixes Icelandic fixings with present day culinary methods. The tasting menu develops with occasional contributions, displaying the best of neighborhood produce in a contemporary setting.

KOL Café: Carrying worldwide style to Reykjavik's eating scene, KOL Eatery offers a different menu with impacts from Italy, Spain, and then some. The classy air supplements dishes like barbecued Icelandic sheep and skillet singed icy roast.

d. Bistros and Bread kitchens:

Braud and Co: For a sample of Icelandic cakes and newly heated bread, visit Braud and Co in Reykjavik. This craftsman pastry shop embraces conventional strategies, creating sourdough and cinnamon moves that are essentially compelling.

Bistro Loki: Situated close the notorious Hallgrímskirkja church, Bistro Loki is a beguiling spot to relish conventional Icelandic cakes and baked goods. Attempt their rye bread frozen yogurt, a brilliant combination of sweet and exquisite flavors.

e. One of a kind Eating Encounters:

Icelandic Road Food: Embrace the easygoing side of Icelandic eating with a visit to Icelandic Road Food in Reykjavik. Devour good customary soups, including the famous sheep soup, as you investigate the city.

Particle Experience Lodging's Silfra Eatery: Adventure past Reykjavik to Þingvellir Public Park and experience Silfra Café at the Particle Experience Inn. Appreciate all encompassing perspectives while savoring Nordic-propelled dishes created with nearby and natural fixings.

f. Curious Country Diamonds:

Fjöruborðið (The Fjord Board): Situated in the beguiling coastline town of Stokkseyri, Fjöruborðið is famous for its langoustine feasts. Subside into this private café for a sample of Icelandic friendliness and impeccably pre-arranged langoustines served in different delightful styles.

Humarhöfnin (The Lobster Town): Embrace the seaside feel in Höfn, known as the lobster capital of Iceland. Humarhöfnin permits you to savor the freshest lobster dishes while getting a charge out of all encompassing perspectives on the encompassing fjords.

g. Veggie lover and Vegetarian Choices:

Gló: In Reykjavik, Gló stands apart as a shelter for veggie lovers and vegetarians. This wellbeing cognizant restaurant offers a different menu of plant-based delights, from sustaining bowls to tasty wraps, all created with privately obtained natural fixings.

Kaffi Vinyl: Joining an affection for music and plant-based cooking, Kaffi Vinyl in Reykjavik is a vegetarian bistro and record store. Partake in a comfortable climate while enjoying flavorful vegetarian dishes, including good burgers and imaginative plates of mixed greens.

h. Neighborhood Home bases and Bars:

Kex Inn: Past being a well known inn, Kex Lodging in Reykjavik gloats a dynamic gastropub. Jump into a casual climate, matched with a menu highlighting Icelandic solace food, specialty lagers, and unrecorded music.

Miniature Bar: Lager fans will see the value in Miniature Bar, a specialty brew sanctuary in Reykjavik. With a broad choice of neighborhood and global brews, it's an optimal spot to investigate Iceland's thriving specialty lager scene.

i. Distant Wild Feasting:

Inn Rangá's Eatery: Travel south to Inn Rangá for a remote feasting experience in the midst of Iceland's stunning scenes. This upscale eatery offers a different menu highlighting Icelandic fixings, giving a culinary desert garden amidst nature.

Icelandic Ranch Occasions: For a genuinely vivid encounter, consider eating with Icelandic homestead families through the Icelandic Ranch Occasions program. Share a dinner with local people, getting a charge out of hand crafted dishes and acquiring experiences into rustic Icelandic life.

Chapter 13

Hidden Gems in Iceland:
A Treasure Hunt Through Its Unknown Gems.

Settled inside the enamoring scenes of Iceland, the Unexpected, yet invaluable treasures area uncovers an embroidery of fortunes outside of what might be expected, welcoming brave pioneers to uncover the less popular miracles of this charming country. A long way from the clamoring traveler center points, this local offers a peaceful departure into the immaculate excellence of Iceland's regular marvels.

As you adventure into Unlikely treasures, you'll wind up drenched in this present reality where geothermal natural aquifers call, projecting a warm hug in the midst of the cool Icelandic air. The area is dabbed with lesser-investigated cascades that fountain down tough precipices, their ethereal magnificence intensified by the shortfall of groups.

Cross the winding paths that lead to separated icy tidal ponds, where goliath ice sheets float calmly against a setting of lofty mountains. The aurora borealis graces the night sky with its divine dance, giving a sensational display away from the city lights.

The Unexpected, yet invaluable treasures area is likewise a shelter for natural life lovers, with its immaculate scenes filling in as a safe-haven for exceptional vegetation. Catch looks at Cold foxes, tricky reindeer, and a horde of bird animal varieties as you explore through immaculate knolls and seaside bluffs.

For those looking for social submersion, interesting towns inside the Unlikely treasures uncover a mix of custom and innovation. Draw in with local people, appreciate valid Icelandic cooking, and experience the glow of authentic neighborliness that characterizes this odd area.

In Unlikely treasures, each corner recounts a story, and each step discloses a mystery ready to be found. This local welcomes those with a courageous soul to exchange the natural for the exceptional, promising an extraordinary excursion through the secret fortunes that make Iceland a genuine jewel for those able to investigate past the traditional ways.

Settled in the midst of the tough scenes and stunning view of Iceland lies an unlikely treasure - an area off in an unexpected direction that reveals the nation's fortunes in a manner that goes past the commonplace vacationer trail. This unseen area, away from the clamoring swarms, welcomes voyagers to drench themselves in the legitimate appeal and regular ponders that make Iceland really novel.

1. Húsavík: The Whale Watching Capital
While numerous sightseers run to Reykjavik, Húsavík stays a beguiling town on the northeastern coast, eminent as the whale-watching capital of Iceland. Leave on a peaceful boat excursion to observe grand animals like humpback and minke whales nimbly exploring the Icy waters. The town's beautiful appeal adds to the charm, giving a valid Icelandic encounter.

2. Seydisfjordur: A Serene Fjord Town
For those looking for peacefulness, Seydisfjordur, arranged in the East Fjords, is a secret heaven. This

interesting town, settled inside a fjord encompassed by snow-covered mountains, flaunts beautiful wooden houses and an energetic expressions scene. Investigate the nearby art shops, partake in the serene environmental factors, and witness the staggering differentiation of nature against the lively tints of the town.

3. Þórsmörk: The Valley of Thor

Escape into the core of Iceland's wild by wandering into Þórsmörk, a valley encompassed by ice sheets and mountains. Open by super jeep or climbing, this far off objective offers a genuinely off-the-framework experience. Submerge yourself in staggering scenes, cross icy waterways, and find stowed away cascades as you navigate this immaculate sanctuary.

4. Drangshlíð: A Secret Magma Field

Away from the run of the mill traveler courses, Drangshlíð uncovers a strange scene of old magma fields and greenery covered rocks. The extraordinary landscape gives a powerful encounter, and as you explore the paths, you'll experience stowed away caverns and volcanic arrangements. It's an enthralling look into Iceland's geographical miracles.

5. Vestmannaeyjar: Islands of the Atlantic
Take a ship to Vestmannaeyjar, a gathering of islands off the south coast that rose up out of volcanic emissions. The archipelago offers a mix of normal excellence and a rich social history. Investigate the Eldheimar historical center, which grandstands the effect of a volcanic emission in 1973, and partake in the tough scenes and seabird provinces that characterize these secret islands.

6. Snæfellsnes Landmass: A Microcosm of Iceland
Frequently alluded to as "Iceland in Smaller than usual," the Snæfellsnes Landmass embodies the different magnificence of the country inside a reduced region. From sensational beach front bluffs to famous Snæfellsjökull spring of gushing lava, this locale grandstands the quintessence of Iceland without the groups. Investigate enchanting fishing towns, as Arnarstapi, and be dazzled by the always evolving scenes.

7. The Westfjords: Iceland's Distant Wild

For the daring soul, the Westfjords allure with their far off wild and immaculate magnificence. Fjords cut through the scene, giving a sanctuary to natural life and tranquil scenes. Find stowed away natural aquifers, climb along waterfront precipices, and appreciate the disengagement that characterizes this lesser-investigated district.

8. Laugarvellir: Geothermal Desert garden in the High countries

Adventure into the distant High countries to find Laugarvellir, a geothermal desert garden encompassed by obvious volcanic scenes. Loosen up in normal underground aquifers, embraced by the isolation of the high country wild. The differentiation of the percolating geothermal pools against the rough landscape makes a dreamlike and reviving experience.

9. Borgarnes: Authentic Serenity

Settled on the shores of Borgarfjörður, Borgarnes gives a quiet departure a dash of history. Visit the Settlement Place to dive into Iceland's adventures, investigating the country's rich social legacy. The town's beach front setting, with perspectives on the fjord and mountains, adds a peaceful appeal to your excursion.

10. Djúpavík: Deserted Herring Industrial facility

For a special mix of history and frightful magnificence, Djúpavík, a previous herring plant on the Westfjords, stands frozen in time. Investigate the unwanted production line, witness the rotting leftovers of a past time, and absorb the hauntingly lovely environmental elements. The ruined appeal of Djúpavík recounts a quiet story of Iceland's modern past.

11. Glymur: Iceland's Tallest Cascade

Get away from the groups at the more well known cascades by searching out Glymur, Iceland's tallest cascade, concealed inside the Hvalfjörður fjord. Climb through lavish gulches and cross an exhilarating ravine extension to arrive at this superb fountain. The actual excursion turns into an undertaking, and the prize is a stunning perspective on Glymur diving into the gorge beneath.

12. Heimaey: Volcanic Island Heaven

Investigate the volcanic miracles of Heimaey, the biggest island in the Vestmannaeyjar archipelago.

Visit Stórhöfði, a bluff with all encompassing perspectives, and witness the leftovers of Eldfell's 1973 emission. The island's rough magnificence, joined with its lively birdlife, makes Heimaey a secret heaven in the limitlessness of the Atlantic.

13. Askja: Caldera in the Wild

Set out on an endeavor to Askja, a distant caldera in the Icelandic Good countries. Open by testing streets, this lunar-like scene offers an extraordinary encounter. Wash in the Víti cavity, a geothermal lake inside Askja, encompassed by ruined at this point spellbinding landscape that feels like an excursion to the moon.

14. Grundarfjörður: Kirkjufell's Unexpected, yet invaluable treasure

While Kirkjufell is a notable milestone, the close by town of Grundarfjörður gives a secret viewpoint. Meander along the shoreline, catching special points of the notorious mountain. The peaceful air and beautiful environmental factors make Grundarfjörður a brilliant stop for those looking for a calmer experience with this renowned Icelandic milestone.

Setting out on an excursion through these unlikely treasures offers an embroidery of encounters, from geothermal marvels and verifiable experiences to deserted scenes frozen in time. Iceland's fortunes off in an unexpected direction entice the valiant voyager, promising a more profound association with the country's untamed soul and phenomenal normal excellence.

Chapter 14

Souvenir Shopping in Iceland

Welcome to the captivating universe of trinket shopping in Iceland, where the lively culture and shocking scenes show signs of life in a horde of exceptional remembrances. Iceland, a place that is known for ice sheets, springs, and old stories, offers a gold mine of particular keepsakes that catch the embodiment of this Nordic island. From conventional Icelandic woolens, similar to the notable lopapeysa sweater, to perplexing high quality specialties propelled by Norse folklore, every trinket recounts to a story well established in the country's rich history and normal marvels.

Leave on an excursion through the clamoring markets of Reykjavik or the interesting craftsman shops dissipated the nation over, and you'll find a different cluster of things mirroring Iceland's imaginative creativity. The unpleasant magnificence of volcanic scenes finds articulation in complicated basalt adornments, while the supernatural appeal of Aurora Borealis is typified in hypnotizing craftsmanship pieces and crystal. Past the normal postcards and magnets, Icelandic trinkets encapsulate a combination of contemporary plan and old practices, making them badge of movement as well as windows into the spirit of this uncommon land.

Whether you're attracted to the otherworldly images of the Vikings, the ethereal magnificence of hand-cut Icelandic runes, or the pragmatic tastefulness of regular things implanted with neighborhood beguile, gift shopping in Iceland guarantees a brilliant experience. Go along with us as we investigate the spellbinding universe of Icelandic souvenirs, where each buy turns into an unmistakable memory, a piece of the country's spirit that you can convey home with you.

Woolen Fortunes: Icelandic fleece is famous for its quality and warmth. Search for hand tailored woolen things like sweaters, covers, and gloves decorated with customary examples. These things feature nearby craftsmanship as well as give a comfortable indication of Iceland's crisp environment.

Lopapeysa (Fleece Sweaters): A quintessential Icelandic gift, the lopapeysa is a conventional fleece sweater enhanced with particular examples. Neighborhood markets and specialty stores offer different plans, each with its remarkable story established in Icelandic fables and history.

Icelandic Plan: Investigate shops in Reykjavik for contemporary Icelandic plan things. From home style to dress, these pieces reflect current Icelandic feel. Brands like Ranchers Market and Geysir are known for consolidating custom with a contemporary wind.

Painstaking work: Embrace the appeal of Icelandic painstaking work, for example, hand-cut wooden things, stoneware, and calfskin products. These artworks frequently consolidate images propelled by Icelandic nature and folklore, making them significant and genuine keepsakes.

Icelandic Chocolate: Fulfill your sweet tooth with Icelandic chocolate. Brands like Omnom and Noi Sirius produce excellent chocolates with extraordinary flavors, for example, licorice or ocean salt, adding a scrumptious touch to your gift assortment.

Skyr Items: Skyr, a conventional Icelandic dairy item, has acquired worldwide prevalence. Bring back skyr-based items like sticks, chocolates, or even skincare things mixed with the decency of this Icelandic staple.

Viking-propelled Product: Jump into Iceland's Viking history with keepsakes propelled by its incredible past. Search for things like rune-recorded adornments, drinking horns, or scaled down Viking ships, which give recognition to Iceland's all's Norse legacy.

Icelandic Books: Investigate the scholarly side of Iceland by getting a book from a nearby writer or one roused by Icelandic adventures. English interpretations are broadly accessible, permitting you to dive into the country's rich artistic practice.

Volcanic Debris Items: A few craftsmans make special pieces utilizing volcanic debris, integrating the tough quintessence of Iceland into gems, earthenware production, and workmanship. These things act as a substantial association with Iceland's geographically dynamic scene.

Neighborhood Workmanship: Support neighborhood specialists by buying works of art, prints, or photos portraying Iceland's stunning scenes. These pieces catch the excellence of the nation and make for a significant and outwardly engaging keepsake.

Icelandic Ocean Salt: Reaped from the unblemished waters encompassing Iceland, Icelandic ocean salt is a connoisseur gift. Mixed with the nation's unadulterated and fresh marine flavors, it's accessible in different structures, from conventional pieces to imbued assortments like birch or Cold thyme.

Blue Tidal pond Magnificence Items: Bring the restoring impacts of the Blue Tidal pond home with skincare items got from its mineral-rich waters. Facial coverings, creams, and shower salts offer a spa-like encounter and make for sumptuous, spa-motivated gifts.

Puffin-themed Things: Puffins are notable occupants of Iceland, and you'll find different keepsakes including these enchanting birds. Search for puffin-themed dress, magnets, and rich toys, making a capricious and charming sign of your Icelandic experience.

Reindeer Items: Reindeer wander unreservedly in specific pieces of Iceland, and items produced using reindeer calfskin or prongs are novel and legitimate keepsakes. Things like wallets, keychains, or even beautifying pieces feature the association between Icelandic culture and nature.

Melodic Tokens: Iceland's music scene is energetic and mixed. Bring back a piece of this melodic culture with Icelandic music Discs or vinyl records highlighting neighborhood specialists. On the other hand, think about customary Icelandic instruments as a novel keepsake.

Rune Stones: Embrace the supernatural side of Icelandic culture with rune stones. Cut with antiquated images, these stones are accepted to hold profound importance. They make for fascinating and emblematic mementos, associating you to Iceland's verifiable roots.

Handwoven Materials: Customary Icelandic winding around procedures produce lovely materials. Search for handwoven scarves, decorative liners, or covers including multifaceted examples motivated naturally and old stories. These materials grandstand the expertise and imaginativeness of nearby specialists.

Icelandic Alcohol: Test Iceland's one of a kind spirits and bring back a container of Brennivín (Icelandic schnapps) or other privately delivered mixers. The particular flavors catch the pith of the locale, giving a sample of Icelandic culture.

Icelandic Ponies Memorabilia: Iceland's strong and one of a kind variety of ponies is praised in different keepsakes. Look over horse-themed craftsmanship, models, or even little dolls as a beguiling indication of these cherished Icelandic sidekicks.

Aurora Borealis Keepsakes: Remember the entrancing Aurora Borealis with gifts motivated by Aurora Borealis. From artworks to dressing enhanced with dynamic tones, these things catch the enchantment of Iceland's night sky.

Keep in mind, whether you're walking around the roads of Reykjavik or investigating the open country, Iceland offers a different scope of gifts that go past the regular knickknacks, permitting you to bring back home a piece of this charming island.

Chapter 15

Tips and Essential Information for Travelers Visiting Iceland

Iceland, with its powerful scenes and dazzling excellence, is a fantasy objective for some explorers. Whether you're pursuing Aurora Borealis, drenching yourself in the dynamic neighborhood culture, or wondering about normal marvels like cascades and springs, here are fundamental tips to upgrade your Icelandic experience.

Welcome to the captivating place that is known for Iceland, where powerful scenes, lively culture, and warm neighborliness meet to make a really extraordinary travel insight. As you leave on your excursion to this Nordic island, our aide means to furnish you with fundamental tips and data, it isn't simply paramount yet additionally consistent to guarantee your investigation. From the ethereal Aurora Borealis to the flowing cascades and geothermal marvels, Iceland allures with its normal ponders, and we're here to direct you through each step of your experience.

Weather and Clothing: Iceland's weather can be unpredictable. Pack layers, waterproof clothing, and sturdy footwear. Even in summer, temperatures can vary, so it's wise to bring a mix of warm and cool-weather attire.

Currency and Payment: The Icelandic currency is the Icelandic Króna (ISK). While credit cards are widely accepted, it's advisable to carry some cash for smaller establishments and remote areas.

Language: The official language is Icelandic, but English is widely spoken. Learning a few basic Icelandic phrases can enhance your experience and interactions with locals.

Transportation: Renting a car is a popular option for exploring Iceland's diverse landscapes. Ensure your vehicle is suitable for the terrain, especially if venturing into the highlands. Public transportation is available, but schedules can be limited in remote areas.

Safety Precautions: Iceland is known for its low crime rate, but natural elements can pose risks. Always adhere to safety guidelines, especially when exploring glaciers, hot springs, and geysers. Stay informed about weather conditions and road closures.

Local Cuisine: Try traditional Icelandic dishes like lamb, seafood, and skyr (a yogurt-like dairy product). Keep in mind that dining out can be expensive, so consider budgeting accordingly.

Water Safety: Iceland boasts pristine water sources, and tap water is safe to drink. Reduce plastic waste by carrying a reusable water bottle and refilling it as needed.

Daylight Hours: Iceland experiences long daylight hours in summer and short days in winter. Plan activities accordingly, and consider the Northern Lights if visiting during the darker months.

Hot Springs Etiquette: If you're indulging in Iceland's famous hot springs, be mindful of local customs. Shower before entering, and don't bring any glass containers.

Photography Opportunities: Iceland is a photographer's paradise. Be sure to have a good camera and spare batteries to capture the breathtaking landscapes, waterfalls, and wildlife.

Road Conditions: Iceland's roads can vary from well-paved highways to gravel roads. Check road conditions and weather updates regularly, especially if planning to explore remote areas. Renting a 4WD vehicle is recommended for certain routes.

Wildlife Awareness: Iceland is home to diverse bird species and seals. Respect wildlife habitats, keep a safe distance, and follow guidelines for bird-watching to minimize disturbance.

Camping Rules: Camping is a popular way to experience Iceland's outdoors. Familiarize yourself with camping regulations, use designated campsites, and leave no trace to preserve the pristine environment.

Emergency Services: Save emergency contact numbers in your phone and familiarize yourself with the location of the nearest hospitals or healthcare facilities. Iceland's emergency number is 112.

Internet Connectivity: While urban areas have good internet connectivity, some remote locations may have limited access. Consider purchasing a local SIM card or portable Wi-Fi device for continuous communication.

Cultural Respect: Respect local customs and traditions. Ask for permission before taking photos of people, and be mindful of cultural nuances to ensure positive interactions with the Icelandic community.

Aurora Borealis Viewing: If witnessing the Northern Lights is on your agenda, venture away from city lights for optimal viewing. Check Aurora forecasts, and be patient, as the lights may not always be visible due to weather conditions.

Travel Insurance: Ensure you have comprehensive travel insurance covering medical emergencies, trip cancellations, and unexpected incidents. This provides peace of mind and financial protection during your journey.

Opening Hours: Icelandic businesses may have shorter opening hours, especially in rural areas. Plan your activities accordingly, and check the opening times of attractions, restaurants, and services.

Geothermal Areas Safety: When exploring geothermal areas, follow marked paths to avoid dangerous areas with hot springs and geysers. The ground may be fragile, and stepping off designated paths can pose risks.

Celebrate Icelandic Holidays: Participate in local festivities if your visit aligns with Icelandic holidays. It's an excellent opportunity to immerse yourself in the culture and traditions of this unique island nation.

Book Accommodations in Advance: Especially during peak tourist seasons, it's advisable to book accommodations in advance. This ensures you have a place to stay and allows for better budgeting.

Visit the Blue Lagoon Responsibly: The Blue Lagoon is a popular attraction, but booking tickets in advance is crucial. Respect the rules, shower before entering, and avoid getting your hair wet if it's colored, as the minerals may affect it.

Time Your Visit to Popular Attractions: To avoid crowds, plan your visits to popular attractions like the Golden Circle early in the morning or later in the evening. This allows for a more intimate experience with Iceland's iconic sites.

Learn About Iceland's History: Enhance your trip by learning about Iceland's rich history, folklore, and sagas. This knowledge adds depth to your exploration of historical sites and cultural landmarks.

Stay Informed About Volcanic Activity: Iceland is geologically active, and volcanic eruptions can impact travel plans. Stay informed about any ongoing volcanic activity and follow safety recommendations provided by local authorities.

Pack Essentials for the Highlands: If you plan to explore the Icelandic Highlands, pack essentials such as a GPS, extra fuel, food supplies, and a reliable map. The highland roads are challenging, and preparation is key for a successful journey.

Utilize Local Advice:Interact with locals, seek their advice, and embrace the Icelandic way of life.

Locals can provide valuable insights, recommend hidden gems, and share authentic experiences.

Explore Beyond Reykjavik: While Reykjavik offers urban charm, Iceland's true beauty lies in its natural wonders. Venture into the countryside to explore waterfalls, glaciers, and quaint villages, experiencing the country's diverse landscapes.

Practice Responsible Tourism: Respect the environment and adhere to the principles of responsible tourism. Stay on designated paths, avoid disturbing wildlife, and minimize your ecological footprint to contribute to the preservation of Iceland's pristine nature.

Aurora Photo Tips: If photographing the Northern Lights, use a sturdy tripod, a wide-angle lens, and a low ISO setting for clear and vibrant images. Familiarize yourself with night photography techniques to capture this awe-inspiring phenomenon.

Plan for the Midnight Sun: During the summer months, when the Midnight Sun graces the sky, plan activities that take advantage of the extended daylight hours. This is a unique opportunity for round-the-clock exploration.

By incorporating these additional tips into your travel plans, you'll have a comprehensive guide to navigating the enchanting landscapes and cultural richness that Iceland has to offer. Enjoy your Icelandic adventure!

Printed in Great Britain
by Amazon